Do You Know God?

By

Kenneth E. Dobbin

Foreword

By

Paul A. Whiteford DM.

Do You Know God?
by Kenneth E. Dobbin

Printed in the United States of America

ISBN 1-594670-47-1

Xulon Press
www.XulonPress.com

Xulon Press books are available in bookstores everywhere, and on the Web at www.XulonPress.com.

Table Of Contents

Who Needs To Know God? 15
You Make The Choices In Life 29
Your Life And The Race Set Before You. 41
You Need A Plan. 51
Tools To Study With..59
Bible Study, Where Do I Start?...............................69
Learning To Think In A Godly Fashion. 83
What Is Success In Life?...93
Part Two, Going In God's Strength. 101
Giving A 110%. 105
Confronting Life When It Doesn't Go Right. 117
Your Influence And Being Persuasive. 129
Putting Ethics Into Your Character.......................143
Living By Faith. 155
Making Binding Agreements That Work. 167
Enduring Verses Shrinking Back. 179
Standing Firm In The Heat Of The Battle. 191
The Commitment To Be Effective. 203

Handling The Risks In Life. 215
Paralyzed By What May Happen. 229
God Is With You 24—7. 239
Talking To Your Heavenly Father. 249
Associating With Friends And Family Of God. ..259
Do You Know God's Will For Your Life? 271
About the Author...281

Acknowledgments

I want to thank those who have taken time to help me in my struggle during the time I wrote, "Do you know God." First, I want to thank God for his help to develop my writing skills. He was my constant companion who gave me the plan and the ideas in the book and the friends I needed to encourage me.

Next to God, My wife, who has been at my side with her advice, her love, and understanding. Yet, I know that she spent many hours by herself while I was busy at the keyboard. Thank you, honey.

To Jack Purdy, who gave me a critical review, suggestions and encouragement. To Ernie McFarland who read portions of the book and gave a fair assessment. To Nancy McClurg, Roberta Simpson, the members of my church, Peter Miller and other pastors I associate with, and many of my friends at work. In all, about 75 people who have helped me during this time. Finally, the least I could do is to thank a nameless sweet woman who would love to read your palm but can't wait to read the book. Thank you one and all.

Foreword

All around our house we have Polaroid snapshots of doorknobs, lampshades, light fixtures, handrails and other odd looking pictures. My son, who is developmentally disabled, loves to take pictures. One of his favorite things to do is to point the camera towards his open mouth and photograph his own tongue sticking out! While his parents get a kick out of it, in terms of photography it leaves a little to be desired to say the least.

My son has yet to get the big picture. He doesn't take pictures of the whole horizon. He doesn't get the concepts of landscape, perspective and context. He takes pictures of body parts, doorknobs and fixtures, but not a house with a sunrise coming over the hill. He simply doesn't get the big picture.

It is absolutely critical for us to keep the big picture in view. Too often our theological discussions are like my sons Polaroid pictures; the landscape, the context, the big picture is lost because the focus is on a small part of something much bigger and more meaningful. Lampshades are important, they make for a much more pleasing light source and add beauty to the décor of the house, but frankly I do not really enjoy looking at pictures of our living room's lampshades!

What I am getting at is this. We need to pull the camera back and get the big picture. Not that details are unimportant, but details without perspective and contextual connection can become meaningless, or even grotesque (like a photograph of a popsicle-red tongue)! But if we step back and get the big picture everything makes more sense and is more appealing.

As you take Do you know God? into your hands and begin reading be sure to get the big picture and not lose perspective by focusing exclusively on the small details and parts of this book. The focal point for the big picture is God's love. Certainly God is more than love, but He is never less! The Bible says, "God is love" (I John 4:8, 16). And this simple but powerful revelation of the nature of God enables us to make sense of the parts. It is the big picture perspective that keeps us from confusion and distortion. It is the horizon against which every doctrine must be viewed. God's love is the landscape that connects the details of His revelation with its purpose and makes the big picture appealing and beautiful.

Why did God create the world in the first place? Because "God is love." Love cannot exist in isolation. Love must be revealed. Love must be expressed. Giving and receiving love is impossible apart from creation. God is love, therefore "In the beginning God created the heavens and the earth" (Genesis 1:1)! God is love, therefore "God created man in his own image, in the image of God he created him; male and female he created him" (Genesis 1:27)! Having created man in his own image with all of its capacities for giving and receiving love the Lord said, "It is not good for the man to be alone" (Genesis 2:18)! The details of creation are not unimportant, but in all the discussions of "how" the world was created, if we are not careful we can lose perspective by taking too many pictures of lampshades and not stepping back far enough to ask the big picture questions of "why" the world was created. In my view the big picture answer is "God is love!"

Someone may object however, "If God is love then why does he command and demand so many things?" Focusing on the individual commands and demands of the Bible may cause some to distort the big picture. If we can get more of the horizon in the photograph we can easily understand that a God who is by nature love could not possibly be unconcerned with how the objects of his love live their lives. If my daughter doesn't come home from school as expected because she decided to go her own way and play with a friend, I as a father can be expected to be disappointed and upset by her actions. Why? Is it because she broke one my rules? Well, yes she broke my rules and I don't like that, but the big picture explanation is that I love my kids!

I don't want to see them kidnapped, injured, or lost! Rules are an expression of my love for my kids! Real love is not permissive and God is real love! Love is not god, God is love. If "love" is god, god becomes an abstract quality that is permissive and ultimately impersonal. But God is personal and his nature is love. A love that cares deeply about the welfare, whereabouts, and destiny of his beloved creation! In my view the big picture answer is "God is love!"

A despairing person battling temptation might ask, "Why didn't God just create me so I would automatically believe and automatically obey the Lord?" And to be sure when the focus is on a particular part of this problem it can be very hard to make sense of it all. But if we can pull our perspective back and get the big picture for a moment, the answer again is "God is love!" Real love must be free to choose. Machines do not love. I can record my voice saying "I love you" and play it over and over again, but no matter how many times I hear it I cannot experience love from a machine recording, or a robot that always does what I want it to do. The only way we know love is when it is freely expressed by someone not something!

God created us to receive and give love. The only way that is possible is also creating the real possibility that freedom may choose against love.

But why did Jesus come to the earth and suffer on the Cross? The Bible tells us that the big picture answer is "God is love." "For God so love the world that He gave His one and only Son, that whoever believes in him shall not perish but have eternal life. For God did not send his Son into the world to condemn the world, but to save the world through him" (John 3:16-17). Humanity was created with the required freedom to receive and give love, but unfortunately from the very beginning to this very day we have chosen poorly. Why the Cross, the blood, the tomb? Because God is love! Love found a way to remedy the devastating damage sin did to God's plan for us to receive and give love. Because God is love, He cannot permissively let self destructive and relationship ruining behavior go without consequence or remedy. The love of God was focused in the person of Jesus in order to restore the original intention of Creation! To redeem us for himself so that the relationship God planned from the beginning could be lived and experienced.

His love connects everything! If you are struggling with a particular dimension of knowing God, step back and get the big picture. God is love! His love is bigger than the horizon we can see, but step back far enough to get a good landscape perspective of how God's love makes all of the details of God's revelation make sense. Get his amazing love for you in full view!

Kenneth Dobbin is one of those guys that every pastor needs to keep him on his toes! Discussing theology with Ken almost feels like it could become a contact sport! Yet even when we disagree significantly, I never get the idea that Ken is off focus when it comes to the big picture! Ken loves the Lord and offers this book as a resource for others to experience the big picture truth "God is love!" In fact, *Do you know God?* is itself an expression of love.

Paul Anthony Whiteford, D. Min.

CHAPTER 1

Who Needs To Know God?

Do you know God? This question may be blunt, but it has a life and death answer that you should know before you die. In so many ways, God tells you that he exists. In spite of who you are you can feel the heat of the sun, gaze at the beauty of a rainbow, and hear God's name spoken. The way things were made makes you wonder who made all of this and how did it come into being? Questions like these make it clear, God made all that you can see, hear, smell, and touch.

Man knows that God exists by the things he made and still fails to see him as the one who rules the world. Man opposes God on the issue of authority more than all the other reasons. Though man is of the world, he or she tells their creator that they want a life of their own? They want to run their life as they see fit and use the things God has made without giving God the respect due him. Think for a moment, would you let anyone in your home that has no respect for you or the things you own? There is also a fallacy in man's beliefs when they ignore God's authority in this life but want to go to heaven when they die where God is in charge. They are in charge of their life more than they think but with that attitude they are a threat to God's authority. Still, man needs to understand that God is an eternal being and he will still be in charge when this age is over. The person, who wants nothing to do with God, will have his wish.

The question as posed may need to be modified. Do you know God or about him? In the US, the Barna Research Group gathers data that shows four out of ten Americans go to church each week (www.barna.org). Ask the six that are not in Church if they know God? Some think that all they have to do is to live a good life to go to heaven. Some know that God lives in heaven and they don't have time for him. The rest speak with their eyes and ears shut to the matter and assume more than they should. The idea that you could know God seems foolish to six out of ten men in the US. However, for the Christian, it is plain to see that the world lacks a need to know God. Take a look at your life from God's perspective. God wants to know you but on the day Christ meets you at the heaven gate, is it possible that he could say. "I don't know you." Matt 25:12. The result would be devastating to you. The need to know God has changed and so has the question. "Do you know God" or just how well do you need to know God?

You may want to take stock of your life and do a reality check. Where does God work? What is his job? Why did God make the world? What kind of plans does God have for you? Why does God hate sin? Does Christ have a role to play in your life? Where do you fit into God's plan? Does God want to rule your life? Are heaven and hell real? If so, where will you go when God reviews what you have done with your life? The questions can go on and on, so take some time to think. Did the answers give you a reason to know God? These 10 questions deal with your relationship to God and your future. The answers may help you to make the right choice and live in such a way that allow God to open his arms and welcome you to his home.

How do I know God?

You may ask, is there a way to know God? The way to know God is simple, spend time with him and ask him to do things for you. Friends who talk to each other know each other. Once, you know them, you will not only know where they work but what he or she does on their job. You will know the plans they have and what they desire out of life. You will see they have a life much like yours, cluttered with pictures on the wall and memories that go back to their youth. As a friend, you may share many of those memories.

Relationships are two sided. To know anyone, you must use your time to be with them and be willing to share your life. When alone with your friends, you will see the way they think and the way they live. Your ways may be offensive to them and to show your desire to keep them as a friend you may have to change your habits. The things you do for each other gives you a relationship that will last the rest of your life.

Money does not enter your mind when it comes to those you love. Freely, what you have is theirs to use. To be a friend, you give your time and share your belongings with them. You do things that serve your friend's need, which shows how you feel about them. You're there for them any time of the day ready to give help. Doing favors for them builds a relationship that money can not buy. You make your friends feel important and that makes them want to keep you as a friend.

Christian's who want to please God do as Paul wrote. "Find out what pleases the Lord." Eph 5:10. God will talk to you when you read the Bible and you speak to God when you pray. In your prayer, you tell God what you need. Doing the will of God shows that you rely on his word and use your skills to serve him, knowing no harm will come to you as a result of your trust. Thus, when you know how to please God, you can do what he expects of you.

The Christian has God as his father. The man who knows God knows his plan and lives by his faith in God. He gave his life to God when he asked God to save him and gave an oath to obey him. That oath gave God the hope that you wanted to be his son. God adopts you as a son and since God is a spirit, you are born again. This birth speaks of when you are born in the spirit realm. It's then that God opens your eyes and ears to the spirit realm and gives you a new way of life. God's son may live his life in the world but the spirit of God guides him.

A father's need changes his child's life, so the question changes with it. Do you know God well enough that you need to seek him?

What is God's plan?

God is building a kingdom of kings and priests out of men like you. To train you, God gave you the right to rule your life on earth. God lends his help to the humble and will show you how to avoid evil that can rule your life. You may not know that sin robs you of the power to rule your life. God says, "Sin desires to have you, but you must master it." Genesis 4:7. Therefore, you are a slave of your choices. Because sin leads to other events that will force you to sin again, you are a slave to sin. God needs leaders for his kingdom that are free to rule? To meet that goal, God has a plan to teach you how to make the choices that will allow you to rule.

> "Do not let this Book of the Law depart from your mouth; meditate on it day and night, so that you may be careful to do everything written in it. Then you will be prosperous and successful. Have I not commanded you? Be strong and courageous. Do not be terrified; do not be

> discouraged, for the LORD your God will be with you wherever you go."
>
> Josh 1:8-9.

Above is a step by step plan to show you how to have success in life. God has an abundant life and is showing you the way he lives so you can have that kind of life. He tells you to use all of his ideals, then he shows you how to approach life with that plan. God expects you to be a son that looks and acts like him and use his principles. However, your desire to be like him takes effort on your part to work God's plans. This changes the question again. Is your life worth the effort to work God's plan?

Where do I fit in God's Plan?

You may think that your fate was set before you were born, but God does not want anyone to perish and would prefer that you repent. With that in mind he gave you the right to choose your destiny in life. God has offered a plan for you that you can accept or reject. The truth is you have a choice, you can say no to Satan as easy as you can to God. You can live in sin and let sin control your life, but that will seal your fate as well. God said that his truth would set you free to serve him if you so choose. God set before you, the choice of life and of death and he begs you to choose life so that you and your children will have life. That leaves you with a choice to make.

Your relation with God changed when you heard the truth. You made a choice to serve God when you gave your life to God. However, is a choice complete when it is not acted on? Your choice to obey God changed the direction of your life but it is a choice that you need to act on. To this end, God relies on the hope that he can teach you how to make good choices.

God's word gives the proof that his methods work but to test his word you must try it out to see if it makes your life any better. You will have the proof you need after you have tried to live by God's word. God lets you be the judge of his word so will you try to live his way again. When life's trials come on you God wants you learn how to deal with life with his word. God will help you make the right choices that shape your life and let you have your dignity. God gave you his principles to make choices from and he wants you to rely on him.

The choice is now in your hands. The trouble is that you can know how to make a good choice, yet when you make a choice, you prefer what seems best for you at that moment? The result is that you do what you gain the most from. Most men and women on earth do not know that God has planned for you to prosper. He wants to show what your future can be like. In spite of this, God is told that he can rule the world, but not anything of I own.

The Christian wants the world to know that Jesus is Lord. Christ gave his life to set you free from the grasp sin has on you. He made you an heir to his kingdom by giving you the rank of a son. Then this gift of life was sealed by God's spirit to help you live a holy life. All that Jesus has done for you will make you shout, "Jesus is Lord."

The question, "Do you know God", needs to be revised. Do you need a motive to know God?

An incentive to know God?

Make a mistake and everyone knows it but who gets the credit if you do the job right? Bad news travels faster than light so that every one knows who screwed up at work. Is it possible for you do every job right? Life is such that you are human and subject to error. God is willing to show you how to live with a plan and methods that works with results that won't haunt you later in life.

God uses methods that have a feasible way to reach your goals and will show you real to life ways to live. Learn what God has done and then go to work with an eye on the goal. With an eye on the goal you can aim your life for heaven one day at a time. You will know that when you obey God that he will do more than pat you on the back. God will have you soaring with the eagles when you please him.

How to achieve God's goal.

Do you know that God says that you need to be strong? Your skills are like the strands of a rope that make you strong. You increase your chances of achieving your goals when you use all your skills to do a job. It takes more than one strand to make a rope that can lift a ton off the ground. Strength has many attributes and many types of skills will make you stronger. To be strong you must use the sum of your skills in harmony with what you are doing.

Do you gain more from life when you put your all on the line? Christ had life in abundance and he gave all he had to make man right with God. Though he was without sin he became sin and his death was the price that God demanded to atone for your sin. Can you then put all you have on the line as Christ did for you? You only have one life to give and God wants the best you have.

God wants you to use his strength for your goals, but you must not abuse the rights of men. The value and rights of man are upheld by the way that you treat them. Those who live as if their choices did not affect others, rob men of their dignity. Men need to be treated with respect and know that they have honor. You must use a set of ethics with the men in your life to be just and right with God. God will show you the way to live with traits that you need for a good life.

For day to day life, faith is the power you have to rely on. Your faith in God gives you the strength to live when the world says, no you can't. Hearing God speak to you will help you to act with the idea that you can do whatever he tells you to do. Let's face it, God's word puts a fire in your belly that lets you see the impossible as a done deal. Faith gives you the courage to use your skills with God's help. Your trust in God keeps your life strong and the result of your trust helps you be a doer of his word.

Influence is a power to alter the way you think and act. God's word says that Christ died on the cross for your sin while Satan says it's all a hoax. Whom you trust will shape the choices and the beliefs you have. The delusion of sin is strong when you see man sin and indulge his life with it. Your eyes see the lie as truth but the influence of God's word puts the flame of the lie out. Those you trust are your closest friends and they have the power to affect what you believe and what you do.

Courage is the manager of your skills but it is not blind to the risk you face. This is a frame of mind that lets you out perform your peers. You need to see the risks of your life as a problem to conquer and a task that you can excel at when you do it. Courage puts your mind to work to use your skills for any a job that you are not at ease doing it or have not done before. This trait sets your mind on the job that you have to do and then finds a way to do them. You may have knees that knock and the lump in the throat, but the job will get done.

Who opposes God's plans?

Fear is the tool of Satan that will show you the risks and why you can't do them. The finger of fear points at the harm you face. These fears have no basis of truth but it is a belief that by doing God's will you will get hurt. Fear is one thing that defeats the saint before the battle starts because fear will make you hide. God says you have no one to fear but the one that can throw you into the fire of hell.

Your plan will work without a hitch when you draw them up, that is until you put your plan to work.

That is when you find that others have plans of their own. Most of the time, people toss a monkey wrench in your plan. From them you hear oops, oh no, and oh my God what have you done. Those words told you that you have a mess to fix and give you a strong desire to ring the necks of those who made it. Instead God asks that you pray for them and work your way through the mess, relying on his help.

What is it that keeps God's plan from working in your life when that plan worked for Christ and he overcame the world? Christ was in harmony with God for he did the will of God and spoke the words God gave him, then paid the price for you. However, you toss the monkey wrench of sin into your life with the choices you make. You shape your destiny and rebel from the things God tells you to do. You rule your life and live by the choices you make, but did you know that sin is a choice. Sin slips into your life by bad choices, but you can be right with God by using the plan God has given you to rid your life of sin.

God has a rival with a plan of his own, he is a thief and a liar known as Satan. God tossed him to the earth like trash when Satan failed to take his throne. Filled with rage, Satan is out to harm the apple of God's eye. Satan wants to make you a slave to sin in his kingdom but he rules by deceit. Satan wants all God has, and you stand in his way.

How do you defeat a thief and a liar, whose goal is to stop you from doing God's will? God tells you how to punch a hole in Satan's bag of air. Your trust in God is needed to submit to God. When you yield to God, God does his part and Satan will run for his life. God demands that you live right in his eyes and when you do, you will over come the world.

God does not want you to live in terror for it will paralyze your spirit. Fear lets you assume the worse by letting panic have control of your mind. Why bother to tell others the good news when they do not care what you have to say? You now think it is a waste of time and soon lose the desire to do God's will, because you know they will laugh at you. God does not want you to back off, so take time to think. Who or what is behind your thoughts and ideas that stop you from doing God's will?

God said that no matter where you go he will be with you. What more can you ask of God? God will be with you to help resist Satan, when you need him. Thus you have the help of God on demand to do all that is written in God's plan. The question changes again. Do you know God is in you and that you can ask for his help?

My Goal

For the last 20 years God has been working with me to change the choices I make. He gave me the faith to write a book after failing English in high school. God has taught me to do my best, so I want you to see this point. I am only a sample of what God can do with you. God is using my life to glorify him and, in doing so, to tell you that he loves you.

When I do a job I want to do it well, so I set my goals high. God has worked with me to make his ideas known to you. I set a goal for this book to be like the Bible. One that will set the world on fire for God. I hope that you will read "Do you know God" many times. However, take time to ponder the points made in the book, as some of the ideas may be heavy in places. I asked God for his help so that the men and women of the world would desire to know him in a new and fresh way. God inspired me and he deserves the glory for "Do you know God."

What more can I say? "Do you know God" was a step of faith on my part. I'm out on that limb, sawing on the tree side. I know that God has his hand on the saw next to my hand. I know God is so good, should I fail in life or the limb snaps, I know that I will fall into his hands no matter what happens.

CHAPTER 2

You Make The Choices In Life

Life is a question of who has authority when you can rule your life as you like but anyone can tell you what to do. You can only rule your life when you learn to deal with the things that affect your life. It comes down to this concept, you are told to fill out the form, the bank tells you to sign here, and the cop says pull over. Then you go to church to find out that God says you need to repent. These are the terms of the authorities over you and the demands that you need to yield too. You may not like the rules but you can live by their rules when you want to. In most cases, their rules tell you what they need from you so they can serve your needs. When you fail to do what they want you learn too late, or the hard way, that you don't get what you want.

The life God asks you to live is not easy but you don't want to be too late to agree with his demands. God asks that you seek him while he may be found and then draws you to Christ by his cross so you can choose life. Those who ask for life need to be worthy of that gift and should change the way they think and act. No one in his or her right mind wants to go to hell, but being too late tells the story of neglect and a lack to satisfy God's need. God's plan has a simple plan for you to go to heaven, but you need to live by his laws and show the grace of God to the world.

The world knows how to serve the needs of self, but a king serves the needs of others. In God's eye you are his son and he will teach you to rule as a king. God knows that you need love and respect, thus he lives by this rule, "Do to others as you would have them do to you." Luke 6:31. Christ is the king that showed you how to live by denying his own life to ransom yours. Christ came to die for your sin and dying he served your way to be right with God. The choice is in your hand and that choice will shape your future. That choice is to deny your needs to serve God or gain the world to lose your soul.

Americans are free to live as they see fit when they obey the laws of the land. Laws tell its citizens what they can not do and places limits what they can do. The same is true of God, because his law places limits on your life. Since God owns the world and the life on it, he has the right to rule everything pertaining to the earth as he sees fit. God gave man this command: "Obey me, and I will be your God and you will be my people. Walk in all the ways I command you, that it may go well with you," Jer 7:23. You may think that God is telling you how to live, but living by his laws is similar to the way you live now. The difference is the authority you recognize and the laws that you submit to. Living by God's law leads to the life that God wants you to have and shows you how to live with the race of human beings that God created and loves.

Your choices change with life.

Think back to the time when you found the love of your life. This was the time that you came to know them and fell in love with them. You made time and put your life on hold just to be with them, since all you wanted was to be near that person. You got to the point that you could not live without them, so you made a choice that would last a lifetime. You were so in love that the two of you chose to get married.

Up to this point in your relation you saw the good things that drew them to you. Marriage opened a door into your life that you had not seen before. For the first time, after the words "I do," you saw things that they did to change your life. The seat was left up and she sat in the coldest water she could think of, but he could not find his comb for the hair sprays and shampoos. They were not afraid to tell you how and where to put your stuff, which took your freedom and put limits on your life. With their best side no longer in sight it made you wonder, whom did you marry? Your life changed and then you made the choice to make the best of married life.

Marriage is more of a test to know whom you married, as it will take 20 years to know how to please your spouse. In that time the kids will change the rules, school will change the rules and the other events of your life will change the rules even more. Life goes on, but you had to change with the events of your life. What could you do when life changed and you were forced to make more choices? These changes taught you and your spouse to work as a team to raise your kids. Your dreams were put on hold so that the kids could have a better life. If anything, married life teaches you to make a way to agree and work as a team.

Learning to agree

You begged for the toys that you saw in the store when you were a child. Your parents made choices for you when they could afford it. Then dad told you that he agreed with mom and you had to earn your toys. You had the toys you desired but you also had to obey your parents. You found out the hard way that you can want all you want, but you can't have all you want from life.

Working against the methods of whoever is in charge leads to strife. Do things your way and the foreman will tell you to do your job his way or else. Who is the first to say that he or she is not doing their job when their job affects yours? Try to see things from their eyes, because you are not alone in this world, they want a life too. You soon learn that life is better when you agree with those in charge. You can learn to agree with God and obey his laws or you can buck his system and do things your way. Doing things your way will get you into trouble, and like the foreman, God will show you who is in charge. The wise man thinks ahead to the day he expires when he meets God with a final word about how he lived. From God's eye, he saw your deeds as the ideals you have chosen to live by and may put you in conflict with God's demands.

You may not think that you have a choice over death and taxes? This adage is partly true, but you can agree to do things that give you life. You can pay the taxes or let the IRS put you in jail and levy fines. These are the times when it is best to agree with those in charge or they will make your choices for you. Choices are made for you more than you like. While you may not like your options, they still guide the choices you make. God has given you a choice to make concerning your life, but you have to choose life or he will make a choice you will not like.

Making choices.

God chose to give you the control of your life when he made you. From God's point of view you will make many choices in your lifetime to rule your life. Choices are forced on you by the events of your life, but you make life better by the choices you make. The options you have to work with will make some of your choices for you. Your goal has to be worth working for, so you must look at what you have to do. "What are the best options that will achieve what I want out of life?" Questions like these help you to make decisions but of all the options, the one you prefer is the choice you make.

Death is not on the list of things to do nor does it make your life any better. No one in his or her right mind chooses to end his or her life. At death you will go to a realm that God rules and where the choice over your life is in God's hand. God's word says, "Just as man is destined to die once, and after that to face judgment." Heb. 9:27. Dying may be the last thing on your mind but God's word could be the last word you hear. Life is precious but you have to let God know you want his gift of life before you die.

You may like toys but are they practical for the kind of life you want in the long run? It is like drinking beer when it does not fit the life you need. Some say that beer is a healthy food but it does not mix with driving. Beer slows the thinking process and the time that you react, thus its influence can be costly and lead to sin. Your choice must keep your life goals in mind in every choice you make.

The goals you set ensure that you will have more decisions in the days to come. Those goals make plans for your future and shape the life you want to have. Yet to have those goals you must agree to do what you planned to do. Other things creep into your life that affect those goals. However, you have to keep those goals in your mind and make each day count as a step towards that goal.

God given options.

> "This day I call heaven and Earth as witnesses against you that I have set before you life and death, blessings and curses. Now choose life, so that you and your children may live and that you may love the LORD your God, listen to his voice, and hold fast to him. For the LORD is your life, and he will give you many years in the land he swore to give to your fathers, Abraham, Isaac and Jacob."
>
> Deuteronomy 30:19-20.

Life is precious and a gift that only God can give but you have a choice to make within the terms God has given you. God has said that you must choose one of these options, life or death. Since God has the monopoly on life, he is the one you must go to for the life you want. For that life God wants you to listen to his voice, and hold fast to him. "Now this is eternal life: that they may know you, the only true God, and Jesus Christ, whom you have sent." John 17:3.

Men are so busy trying to live life their way that they fail to see a need for God. However, the ruler of the world has given you the choice of life and death. You have a choice to know God or you can ignore the one that can give you life. From God's point of view, any choice you make reflects on the disposition that you use to guide your life. Good and evil are basic roots that guide the way you think, but these qualities are also seen in way you live. God is willing to give you life when you commit your life to him, but it will cost you more to ignore him.

So what is the cost of ignoring God? Have you been out in the sun too long and got sun burned? Have you been burnt so bad that you can not stand for your clothes to touch your skin? The pain from the burn would not let you sleep and the salve you put on only lasts for a second or two. God said that he would give the sun power to sear men of the earth for their wickedness.

Fire and brimstone make hell, real. Brimstone is the yellow ash known as sulfur, found at the rim of a volcano and the odor you smell when you strike a match. Sulfur, when burnt, yields a heavier than air gas that floats just above on the floor of hell. In hell you will lay on the floor in chains and breathe this gas. Sulfur gas acts like water as it robs your body of air by filling your lungs with gas. Then you will cough and gasp for fresh air, but all you will be able to breathe will be more of this gas. The fire of hell will keep you on the edge of death and a state of panic.

The gas will begin to burn inside your lungs but the coughing will make your lungs and body ache. The heat from the sulfur will add to the pain, but then your body will try to shake off the pain. What you do to ease the pain will make the pain worse, for in hell you will have no rest. You are alone and, with no hope, you will give way to panic like you have never known before. If you knew God, you would know that he is harsh on evil and that hell does not have a way out.

On the other hand, life begins when you make the choice to know God and live by his plan. God asks that you commit your life to God and then serve him. This choice lead to a holy life that God demands of you. You are told that heaven has streets of gold, but all that can be said of heaven can not show you the abundant life God is willing to give you. Death, pain, and suffering will be no more for God will wipe your tears away and he will place joy in your heart. By knowing God you can experience what heaven is like before you go home to be with him.

You make the final choice.

The Bible tells you a story of the rich man who went to Christ for advice. Like many men of wealth, he felt he had the money to buy his way into heaven. He wanted to know the way to life but the gift of life was the one thing that his money could not buy. God wanted him to sell what he had and give it to the poor. To God your money has little value and the gift of life is just that, a gift. The Bible has something interesting to say about eternal life. "Now this is eternal life: that they may know you, the only true God, and Jesus Christ, whom you have sent." John 17:3.

Man has always sought a way to live longer. Today, through study, man looks at the causes of death but has to face that fountain of youth does not exist. Man knows that God is a living being who is the origin of the life on earth. God has given eyes that see and ears that hear, but man has chosen to close his spiritual eyes and ears to God even though he is life. The wise man knows that only God can give life and seeks God for that life. For this reason, hell is for those who want life but the cost is too high or they are to busy with life to see a need for God.

Man has the statistics to show that using seat belts can save lives but do all drivers wear seat belts? You can know the truth and not live by it, and you can do the wrong thing when you know the right thing to do. Paul said the same things, "For what I do is not the good I want to do; no, the evil I do not want to do— this I keep on doing." Rom 7:19. Just as Paul had help to sin, you will do the evil you do not want to do. You face an enemy that will entice you to sin with any lie that helps, his cause. If you had the proof to show how many saints made it to heaven you would not be living by faith. The truth is that some think they do not need the safety of the seat belt or God's plan. They have a plan of their own and will get to heaven without God's telling them how.

God has given you the choice when you hear his plan and take his gift or say "no thank you." The truth is, salvation is by the grace of God and it is a gift that God longs to give to you. God holds the exclusive rights on life and drew up the laws that you live by. Trying to get around God's plan won't work, for when the number of saints is complete, you will see him in the sky. "Look, he is coming with the clouds, and every eye will see him, even those who pierced him; and all the peoples of the earth will mourn because of him. So shall it be! Amen." Rev 1:7. For he says, "In the time of my favor I heard you, and in the day of salvation I helped you. I tell you, now is the time of God's favor, now is the day of salvation." 2 Cor 6:2. God wants you to know that before you die, you are the only one who can choose life or say "no thank you."

CHAPTER 3

Your Life And The Race Set Before You

> Therefore, since we are surrounded by such a great cloud of witnesses, let us throw off everything that hinders and the sin that so easily entangles, and let us run with perseverance the race marked out for us.
>
> Heb 12:1.

No doubt, you want to go places in life but God has entered you and your friends into a race for your life. In this race, you have the option to run, yet few know that they are in a race for their life. It begins when you are born and ends when you die, but it has a prize that is beyond anything on earth. Paul saw life as a race unlike all others that had a prize worth running for. God's plan is to share his glory with you and the give you the right to rule with him. God will share the ideals he values most with you and will train you to run, using his skills.

Most people know that sports test the skills of your body but this race tests the skills of your spirit. The plan to win this race is similar to those you use to excel in sports. Paul spoke of making his body a slave to keep his life in shape and to get the best results from his work. To give the best he had, Paul knew that his spirit had to rule his body, so he could obey God. As a spirit-led man you have to set your mind on Christ, then apply yourself to run like him. Paul uses the foot race as a way to bring these points out in the open, so your spirit can go to work.

> Do you not know that in a race all the runners run, but only one gets the prize? Run in such a way as to get the prize. Those that compete in the games go into strict training. We do it to get a crown that will not last; but we do it to get a crown that will last forever. Therefore, I do not run like a man running aimlessly; I do not fight like a man beating the air. No, I beat my body and make it my slave so that after I have preached to others, I myself will not be disqualified for the prize. 1 Cor 9:24-27.

In this race God does not dangle the prize in our face like a carrot stick. You have to aim your life at the goal and rely on the coach to get you there. Your faith in God is a factor that will help you to win because it is the use of your faith that gives your coach the ability to help you. He will help you stay in the race with good advice that will keep you aimed at the goal line. You will be in the winner's circle at the end of your life when you apply yourself to his plan.

What God has planned to do can not be stopped. (Paraphrased Isa 14:24, Prov 21:30). You will soon learn that God keeps his eyes on the goals he plans to achieve. Should you fall, God will show you the steps you need to take and help you get back in the race. God has his eye on you and will not let Satan stop you from grasping the prize when you apply your life to God's plan.

You need a plan?

God has goals that he wants you to carry out similar to company boards that set a basic goal for the year to come. They set feasible goals and let those in lower rank plan how to do them. In God's mind, he has a set number of saints that he needs for his kingdom. Rev.6:11. You now have a goal to achieve but you need a plan so you can walk the streets of gold. God has a plan for everything he does and has a plan for you to run his race. With this plan Christ won his race and it is a plan you can use to satisfy God's goal. Because life is so chaotic, you need a plan that will subdue the world to win this race.

In the world the one who came in first wins the prize but this race is not for speed. Paul said that all the men on earth are in this race and that the race will take you a life time to run. Some have started and others have crossed the goal line but now it's time that you start running in this race. To satisfy the sponsor of this race, you have to make time to run the race and run by his rules.

Paul said, "I do not run like a man running aimlessly; I do not fight like a man beating the air. I do not run like a man running aimlessly." 1 Cor. 9:26. Paul has painted a picture of a man with a huge ego and no plan. The man who beats the air with his fist looks good but he is just going through the motions. His ego tells him that he is a good man in the ring and that he will knock the other boxer out. You can hope you that will win but unless you practice how to box, do not expect to win. This man has not considered that his opponent has a plan to beat him to a pulp in during the fight. Ahab said. "One who puts on his armor should not boast like one who takes it off." I King 20:11.

Why do you need to plan when you are so good at running? You can not run any race with your ego in charge because it still takes more than words to run a good race. You may put on a good show, but those who offer the prize want you to run the race their way. You must agree with the sponsor's plan and run the race by his rules. As you run in life you must follow the game plan that your sponsor and coach lay out and ward off the ideas of those who want to spoil the race for God.

The goal.

In any race, the effort you put forth must be worth the prize up for grabs. Is eternal life worth the effort you must make and the time you have to give? You can't ignore the sponsor and you can't buy or con God out of the prize. If you don't run, you forfeit the prize and if you do run you need a feasible plan. The plan will tell you what you have to do but then you still have to run the race. The prize will go to those in the race as long as they run by God's rules.

Someone said, if you fail to plan, you plan to fail, so then by failing to plan you fail to make your life better. Those who plan know that it takes hard work to achieve their goals. The events of the world will keep your mind off the goal but you have to do the work that God's plan entails. God has said there is nothing new under the sun so what has worked in the past will work today. God's plan has worked in the past, is at work now and will till the day God comes for you.

"The kingdom of heaven is like treasure hidden in a field. When a man found it, he hid it again, and then in his joy went and sold all he had and bought that field." Matt 13:44. This man wanted the goods he found in the field and his mind began to click. The story tells you that he did not own the field and that he did not have the funds on hand. In his mind he drew up a plan to sell all he had to buy the field. He knew he would make a profit by selling all he had to buy that field and knew that the field was worth putting his life's work on the line. He bought that field after he had sold all he had and with joy laid claim to the stash that was now his.

Honey, can you pick up a loaf of bread on the way home tonight? See how easy it was to make a new goal and change your plans, all for a loaf of bread. You have to stop by the store on the way home to get that loaf of bread. Before you left the store you saw snacks to munch on and oh no, another goal. Goals are easy to make but you may be asked what went home in the sack? Goals are easy to make but small things can distract you long enough to take your eye off your main goal. Some of those goals make you loose sight of your needs but you are the one who sets the priority for your goals.

Short-term goals such as the snacks will come and go and you will still have long-term goals. Consider the days of your life like the rungs of a ladder that you have to climb. For that goal you have to climb to the top and you take one rung at a time. Work daily, one rung at a time for your goals. It is written that faith without works is dead and so is your goal without work. Setting goals means you have to learn how to budget your time to achieve them. You have to prioritize your time to use it wisely for the goals you want.

The rules.

God wears a number of hats at the track that is not seen by your eye. He is the sponsor, the coach and the judge; the one who hands you the prize, the one who supplies your tools, the rules, and owns the track you run on. In addition, God sent his only son to pay your fees up front. God wants a good race, thus his word and advice serves as the best way to win the race. For this reason, God made sure that you have a copy of his rules known as the Holy Bible. He expects you to know the rules of his race and run the race by them. God will go the extra mile when you apply your life to his race, as it's how you run the race that pleases God.

There is one name by which you can be saved and one way you can win the race. Rules have the goals of the sponsor in mind, thus the rules put limits on those who run. God is not partial for those in this race and all have to run by the same rules to make the race fair. Take the time to fuse the rules in your mind so you can do all that is written in the book. Then as you apply what you know to the race you will hear those words, "well done my son." The rules are for your good as they make you into a new man that is able to run in the race and not faint. God asks that you give all you can give. In return, he will give the best of what he has. Grace beyond measure and a life without end, a prize that only God can give.

The coach.

Unlike other races this race does not depend on who gets to the goal line first. All the runners will cross the goal line at death, but how you run this race is God's goal. You must avoid the rat race the world is running as the world will lose the race. Only a few will win and those who do have Christ for a coach.

You have two coaches to choose from but only one has a win under his belt. Christ has both the time and a desire to help you run the best you can. His hand is open and ready to strive with you so you can win the race. He knows what lies ahead and will show you how to run. On the other hand some may think of Satan as a foe but he runs by rules that will cost you your life. His real goal is to spoil the race that God has sponsored and will turn on you when you choose to run the race. His dream is to take you out of the race causing you to snub the sponsor. He has his own agenda for the race so the desire you have to win the race is a choice of whom you trust the most.

One coach does not play by the rules and the other is the son of God. His love for you led him to die on a cross that paid your fees. Christ showed his love for you and went the extra mile to see that you win the race. It's not his death that shows that you can win but that God raised him from the dead. This coach has won the prize of the race and is sitting at the right hand of God. God wants you to run this race of your free will but he will twiddle his thumbs until you ask for his help. On the other hand Satan will give you a bum steer because his goal is to drag, push, or pull you out of the race and into the fire.

Run to win.

Men run the race as they see fit but without God they carry a load of sin. That load of sin will stop you from running a good race so God gave you a coach. This coach subdued the world working with God and knows how to run this race. His advice has merit and he knows what you need to do. His insight is what you need so listen to his ideas and seek the value of his wisdom. The other runners may be too busy with life but when you run the race Christ gives the edge you need to win. Thus you should covet his advice and use it to run the race set before you.

The runner who wants to win trains his body and runs with the coach on and off the track. He puts his trust in his coach and gives his all to build his strength for the race. He listens to his coach and does what he advises him to do. You have God's word that you will win when you use his plan but with a previous winner you know you can win.

God's racing team is the best but without Christ as your coach you will feel the agony of defeat. You must know that going the extra mile you have to give 110% of your life to the race. Can you love and trust God with all your heart, mind, soul, and might? From God's sight you only have one shot at eternal life but you need to work with Jesus to win.

Focus on the goal.

Keeping your mind on what you are doing makes you more efficient. At work, those that tell you to keep your mind on the job are talking to the one that controls what you are doing. All too often sin will block your path and stop what you are doing. You are not as apt to sin when you focus your mind on what you are doing. When your mind strays off to other things so does what you are doing. The worries of this life can keep you from being aware of what you need to do. It only takes a second to sin, but that sin will set you back where you began. The world tells you to be alert but keeping your mind on your goals is easier said than done. God tells you to be clear minded and to check what you are doing to make sure you are right with his word.

Prune your thoughts when it is a sprout before they can bud and become a crop. As thoughts grow in your mind you need to make those thoughts conform to the mind of Christ. An evil thought acts like a seed that will grow as a weed in your mind if you don't pull it. To do that you need to rule your mind by checking your thoughts against the word of God. Then exercise your mind by thinking on things that are holy and pure.

God asks you to keep your mind on his word and run on the path his word casts light onto. Sin is crouching at your door; it desires to have you, but you must master it. Gen 4:7. The ways of the world can creep on you fast but God wants you to run this race for your life the way his son did. This race is more for your good than you may think for it shapes the way you think and in time the way you live. That is when you can rely on God to carry you through the trials that you face in life.

CHAPTER 4

You Need A Plan

You know that you are one of God's kids but did you know that you act like your kids do? Your kids do not behave well or act the way you want them too. Your job is to show them how to make good decisions as they grow up. Like you, God is showing his kids some of their choices that will get them hurt or be the cause that they will lose friends. God has a better way for you to live than you have and he wants you to know that the way you want to live can destroy your life. You make it obvious that you have a mind of your own when sin gets you into trouble with your father. God's child is as stubborn as your kids are and like God's child, you guard your right to rule as if it were more precious than life. The right to rule your life is yours as long as you live but God wants to show you how to rule your life a better way.

You did not give up the right to rule your life as you see fit when you became a Christian. When you make Jesus your Lord, you chose to guide your life by his word. Jesus said, "If you love me, you will obey what I command." John 14:15. God wants his kids to be productive and prosper by the laws of his kingdom. The truth is that without hearing what God said, can you obey him?

The way you live is a choice but God wants you to know that you can take part in his plan. If you don't make an effort to find out what pleases the Lord will you not know how to have a productive life in God's kingdom? God wants you to take part in his plan so you may know how to think and act with other beings with his standards. The aim of God's plan was meant to make you into a complete person, one that he is proud to say is his child.

The world you live in differs from the way that God thinks and acts but Paul tells you "to live as children of light." Eph 5: 8. Since you are a child of God's and live in a world that affects your thoughts, God asks that you renew your mind. Then use your mind to think on the things that are right, pure, true, and noble. To do this you must be an avid reader and study God's word to be a workman approved by God. Then you can do your part of God's plan with the belief that God will keep his promises.

The plan has to be done God's way.

The schools you went to and on the job training make your career firm. Being a Christian has on the job training that sends you back to the books to see what God has to say. In other words, goof up on the track and your coach will take you back to the books to show you the basics. This is when he shows you what the rules say, what you need to do and what you should do the next time. This kind of training lets you know what to do when that situation comes up again.

When you go to work for any firm, they show you how their work has to be done. In like manner, God's wants you to use his methods and his ways while you work for his kingdom. When you use the principles of God, you put the rules of the race to work. God is the expert in life and the things he asks of you, will help you live right. The problems come when you neglect the rules to do things your way. God will teach the skills you need and will help you to run the race the way God wants you to.

God's plan.

Once into God's word, you learn that Moses led God's people for forty years. God passed his office to Joshua in front of God's people. Afterwards, the events of that day went through his mind and no doubt he was asking God how he was going to do this job? He knew God's plan for his life was huge and that he could use God's help to lead Israel. You too may ask God how to do the job when God gives you a job to do. God's answer is found in Joshua 1:8-9.

> "Do not let this Book of the Law depart from your mouth; meditate on it day and night, so that you may be careful to do

> everything written in it. Then you will be prosperous and successful. Have I not commanded you? Be strong and courageous. Do not be terrified; do not be discouraged, for the LORD your God will be with you wherever you go."
>
> Joshua 1:8-9.

Wow! Wouldn't you be the talk of the town if you run around with a book in your mouth? From a physical standpoint, it does not make sense that you could speak with a book in your mouth? However, keeping the book of law in your mouth does not make sense from man's eyes, so this has to be seen from God's eyes.

What does God gain from you putting the book of law in your mouth and the reason behind his command? You too learn by the needs you have in your daily life but it's questions like these that help you to learn. Children ask way too many questions as they need to know why and who they are. They may sound dumb to you but any question merits an answer when you don't have the answer. Can you make a sound choice when you do not know who, what, or how? Knowledge helps you to make a choice and when you ask, you want the truth. Putting the book of law in your mouth is your source of truth and in his time the answers you need.

Your spirit has a mouth just as your body has a mouth for food. Your spirit lives by the word of God but your flesh lives on bread that comes from the dust of the earth. God said "you do not live by bread alone but by every word that comes from his mouth." Deut. 8:3. God wants you to use your mouth to put the book of law into your spirit. God said, "By the sweat of your brow you will eat your food." Gen 3:19. Work and eating goes hand in hand and so you have to work for the food that fills the hunger of the body and soul. Go to work, use your mouth to chew the book of law into bits and then swallow it. The point is to get every word that comes from God into your spirit where it will give you the power to live.

Tasting God's word.

Your body and spirit will eat the food that is put into its mouth. So you must choose what you eat by your body and spirit's needs, so a good diet makes sense. Some of the foods you love are not good for you but a diet must nourish as well as fill your needs. You need milk for strong bones as much as you need the milk of God's word to be strong.

Food has a flavor that you can taste. You say yuck to foods that you don't like but say yummy, when you want more. The flavor of the food will give you the desire to eat the food you like. The flavor gives you a hunger for some foods and lets you push others away. This shows that you can forgo a good diet for the taste and fill yourself with junk foods that ruin your diet.

"Taste and see that the LORD is good." PS 34:8. To be strong in the Lord you need the power that is in God's word but to taste God's word you have to put God's word into use. Then stand back to see how things turn out because that is when you will know if God's word has worked for you. The results will tell you if you want to use his word again and as a bonus it may give you something to pass on to your friends. When a like trial comes up in a friend's life, you can say that you found that God's ways worked for you. God will get the glory and you may lead them to Christ.

God's goal.

Paul wrote that the child of God was to think on virtues that God has. The world gives you little to build your character with but the things you put into your Spirit will be what you think on. God has ideals that he wants you to use in your diet of which are things that were true, noble, pure, and lovely. (Phil. 4:8.) These are the broccoli and green beans of God's word that your father wants in your diet. The idea is to select what you put in your mind as you do with foods. The foods of the spirit will set your mind on God and make your spirit strong so you are a man that God can use.

The things in your past will tell you what will work this time when you start a new project. When men tell you what they have done, you will recall the same kind of story you did in your past. You look to your past and share those stories with your friends. They are the war stories of your past, like the fish you caught. The size fish may change each time you tell that story but this tells you that your mind wants you to look like superman.

Doctors use a test to see if you are sane. To do this, the doctor will give you a key word then ask you for the first word that comes to mind. Your reply shows if you are of a sound mind by the words you say. This test also shows that your mind works in a set pattern.

Good and evil have merits that you test for their value in your mind. Some of the ideas of the world are not worth hearing while godly values should be cherished. However, you can digest anything you want to but you have a duty to Christ to cast evil ideas out of your life. Close your mouth to the things that do not please God and weed the evil out of your spirit before it can grow. You select what goes into your spirit, so teach your spirit to say yuck to that kind of stuff. By putting the book of law into your spirit's mouth you will hear ideas that are known to be true, tried and tested. You will make God's values your own and write them on the walls of your heart. The time you dwell on God's word will leave a mark on your soul. Then you will be able to think and act as God does bearing good fruit in all you do.

CHAPTER 5

Tools To Study With

Do you know of a bus, ship, or plane that can take you to heaven? Life is a gift and heaven is the celestial home where God and his family live. Jesus said that many would call him Lord at the last day but to your horror, Christ may send you away saying he never knew you. Does that mean that you could know all about God and not know him? Did you know that you could go to church all your life and not know that you have to be born again? The world has a twisted view of God but the facts of life are that you need to seek God to know the truth.

The goal of the Christian is to go to heaven in the next life and they study the Bible to know what to do. You have made the choice to be God's child and have the goal to live a holy life pleasing to God. To live a holy life you need to know the rules so you can run the race that God expects of you. Going to heaven is a lofty goal but you may want to change your goal to that of knowing God to being known by God. One thing is certain, the words that come out of the mouth of God are choice morsels that nourish the soul.

The Bible.

In the past God spoke to men by his spirit through as many as 30 men to write 66 books in 1400 years. These books were combined into one book that is called the Holy Bible. God used men that came from all walks to write his word. They knew God and were willing to give their time to tell their part of God's plan to you. Today, you can know God as they did from God's word.

"Listen, my son, to your father's instruction." Prov 1:8. "My dear children, I write this to you so that you will not sin." 1 John 2:1. These are the words a father uses to speak to his children just as you may say to your children, listen to me so you won't get in trouble. His word is his bond and with his word God shows you how to live a holy life. You can trust God to explain his word but it has a logic that agrees with the truth. With the truth, God lights the bulb in your loft, turns the key to unlock his word and makes your mind click as you read his word. Take time to seek him for God will speak to you when you open your eyes to see his ways and open your ears to hear his wisdom.

Study will give you a way to solve your trials but it is also a result of thought. Look for a study Bible with the study aids that you need and the items that will help you in your quest for truth. Most study

Bibles have an introduction to each book that acts as the "Cliffs notes" of the book. Think about your needs and the tools that gives the best help to know God. What about the references, do you want them in the column or in the verse? Outlines let you see the books by the topics that are in the book and aids like maps or time lines show where and when the events occur. You will not miss any of these aids until you need them.

Your Study Bible needs to be tough but a Bible that you prize and will be lost without. It does not have to be a Bible that other men see and judge you by. So buy a sturdy one that will survive the fall to the floor, the coffee stains, and one that you can feel free to write on. The idea is to choose one that you will use and fits your need.

An Exhaustive Concordance.

Bibles don't have the room as it would be too bulky or heavy to carry to have a full list of words in it. An Exhaustive Concordance will help you find any word in the Bible and this is one book you will use the most to study God's word. This concordance should be keyed to the Bible version you own. Ask the clerk at the bookstore if one is in print for your Bible as this issue may choose the Bible you use.

God's word teaches more by the trail his word leaves and it links his ideals to your life. This book is the magnifying glass that lets you find the clues he left in his word. Your desire to know of God will add depth to your life and place a picture of God's need in your mind. The need to know God's word in detail shows the love you have for God and the desire you have to be with him. You become the sleuth that follows Christ and as sheep that follows the voice of God with your heart.

Have you heard of the needle in the haystack? At times the Bible is the haystack and the word you need is the needle. The trouble is that you know what the word is but the word you want is one of 740,000 words. The clue word is all you need but where do you begin? Using the concordance helps you to find the word in the mountain of words in the Bible.

The word you are looking for will be found in brief phrase listed from a to z. Each phrase has three parts. First is the location, Second is a brief phrase, and third is a number for the key word. First, find your clue word under its heading then look over the phrases that fit. You may have to look at every word in the list to find a match but it is only a matter of time before you find where the word is hiding.

There are two lexicons in the back of this book but the one you use will rely on the Testament the clue word is in. The Old was written in Hebrew and the New is in Greek. Be sure to keep this in mind, as it may confuse you if you do not. All the words of the Bible have a number so you can find the word by its number in the pertinent lexicon.

The Dictionary.

Long words are a pain in the neck but a dictionary will help you to make sense of the Bible terms.

What are words when they sail over your head or they lock up your mind because you don't know what the word means? Because you live by the word of God, words will have a bearing on your life as the words you heed come from the mouth of God. Without words you would lack a way to say who and what you are. Knowing the meaning of words can be life to you as the words God uses can lift your spirits and light up your day. God has a skill at using words that may seem out of place but are accurate for the topic.

A Bible Dictionary.

This book has a wealth of facts from the men who study the Holy Land. You can use the help of those who study the life and times of the people in the Bible. With the right facts you have a way to look at persons, places, and beliefs of the Bible. It gives you an idea of why, when and how the men of the Bible lived that you may not have seen any other way. Add to these, other visual aids such as maps and charts. With these you can trace the steps of men and see the truth in a factual manner.

Other Resources.

Commentaries are the thoughts of the men that write them. Some talk on blocks of scripture and some are by the verse. These can be an aid when you study for they give you new ideas that you may not have seen. Other forms of commentaries are the ideas of others in the form of books, radio and TV programs and pastoral sermons. When you see or hear them, remember that the ideas and illustrations you hear are from men so be sure to check those ideas with God's word.

Word Expositors such as Vines; tell you how the word is used in the Bible. This aid does a good job to reveal the intent of the word. Vine's is one of many such books.

Great men of the past have kept notes of their studies. Scofield and Dakes are two of the well known notes. Those notes are in the margins of the Bible by that name.

In addition, several Bibles are in the study format. The Open Bible, The Inductive Bible study, The Application Bible, The NIV Study Bible, Nelson's Chain reference Bible, Ryrie Study Bibles are a few of the studies Bibles. Each has a way to study and has ideas that make them special so their user can know God.

There is not enough room to talk on all the reference books. God has inspired the writing of many such books, but God's word is the source of those ideas. Take note of the ideas and then check them against God's word. Prove the ideas from scratch to see that they agree with God's word.

The Computer.

We live in an age when the computer is used as a tool that serves man. This tool has touched the life of every man on earth for it has cut his work in half.

Only man is a slave to this tool for while man does his job the computer does the paperwork. Type in file name and the facts are on the screen before you or you can key in a code for the labels to be printed. Man relies on this tool to save time for fun but this tool can ruin his soul. Like your mind, what you put into it is what comes out of it.

The computer is a tool that can be used as a toy to play the net, music, and games. They can rob you of your time with the fun things of life and be a trap to draw you away from God. In short you can make it into a toy that substitutes for God. Soon the kids will need the Internet as a way to do their homework. Some of the pages on the Internet are not fit for your child to see. Like the TV, how do you control what they see or need to look at? The stuff that ruins your life will find a way to be on your hard drive but you have to rule the use of the computer to keep your family true to God. It eats the time that could be a part of your family life. The programs you put on this device will take you from work that has to be done. Last of all, you can be a hermit by staying on the computer but God does not want you to live your life in that fashion.

A computer or Christian bookstore has a good PC Bible starting as low as ten dollars and as high as 500 dollars. Ask the clerk if you can not find them for it is an easier way to study God's word. Some allow you to build the Bible, as you wish while others come as a package for the cost of the books you need. You will not miss the time it took to turn the pages but with a click, the right page now pops into view. The computer cuts time, the paper you use for notes, and errors you had finding the right places in the book. Finally it takes less time to know God.

A Quiet Place to work.

Do you have a quiet place in your home to be with God? Can you make a place with the frills the Lord allows you to have where you can seek God to your heart's content? Use the dining room table if that is all you have but the kids playing around the house will distract you. The place you choose for your quiet time should be free of activity for you will lose your train of thought to deal with the life that goes on in your home. So plan your quiet time with your family's needs in mind.

Time.

Take the time to listen to God, by reading the Bible but read it slow enough to grasp its truth. Don't skim through the Bible like you surf the Internet or trust those who teach God's word. You can be deceived. Use your time to seek the will of God as you are liable for your choices. Putting God's word in your mouth is the best method to know God and gives you peace of mind that you have done his will.

Time is a tool that you have even when you say that you can't find the time to read the Bible. Sounds like a good reason but it tells the world the priority you have to know God? Stop and think, if knowing God had a real priority, you would make the time to be with God. Using your time to know God is better than hearing the words of Christ say he never knew you.

Time is important to you and you know that there is never enough time for the things you need to do. You make time for fun but that fun can rob you of time you need to spend with God. Like your father, God does not demand that you spend exactly one hour a day with him. You choose the time you need to spend with God for you are different from the rest of God's children. Spend the time you need to be with God to know him because you have to work out your own salvation with God with fear and trembling. The time you need with God depends on your needs and only you know how much time you need with God. However, you should make time for God, a daily habit and govern your time accordingly.

How you spend your time shows God the truth about your life. Look at this promise. "The Lord is with you when you are with him. If you seek him, he will be found by you, but if you forsake him, he will forsake you." 2 Chron 15:2. Being a Christian is not a religion but a personal relationship with God. You will know God by making time to be with him and your strength will be the fruit of your time with God. God needs to be shown that you want to know him, because you want too.

You need to know that too much study will lead to an intellectual view of God. Study is not as much to know about God as it is to have time with God. On the other hand one hour with God is better than hours of study or listening to great men give their views. Being face to face with God will tell you more about the love God has for you than all the knowledge you get from others. However, God has the right to ask more from you, when you spend more time with him.

CHAPTER 6

Bible Study, Where Do I Start?

Starting any job can be hard, all the more, when your boss says. "Sit here." Then he gives you ten steps to show you how to do the job and nothing he said made any sense. If anything, he made the situation worse when he spoke in terms you didn't know. Then he left before you could answer him. You just sit there like an idiot, with no idea of what he said and a job to do that you've never seen or done before. You are in a state of shock wondering what on earth, have you got yourself into? That may be the place you are when you were first saved when those who led you to the Lord, told you to pray, read, and study the Bible. Then they went off and left you on your own.

Taking the first step of any plan is the hardest but working in gray areas that you have never worked in before is hard to do. The first step to any race is to get started, for that you may want to place all the tools you need near by. You may want to set a drink on the table next to you and open your Bible. These tell you that you are ready to spend your time to search God's word to know him and want to be alone with him.

Picking a topic to study may not be as hard as you think, for God is awesome. The idea is to know God and learn how to live from the source of all life. Most Christian's want to know when Christ will return and others want to know how to be healed. You may want to know if what you heard from the word of God are true or find an answer to a question you have. Life is such that the trials you face may provide the topic of study.

Some say that the Bible is Greek to them, this phrase was used a few years ago to show that you had no clue of what was being said. God made you and he knows what you can and cannot do. God has a way with words but he gave you a mind to look at his word and the time to ponder on it. God wants you use your mind, your time, and a desire to know him as a friend. These things make a feasible way to know God and a reason to spend time with God talking about how life affects you.

The Bible is like a puzzle. Instead of having the pieces scattered out on a table the pieces are scattered through out the Bible. To put the puzzle together, you have to compare one piece of the puzzle to another. The piece in Exodus may fit the piece in Romans. To make sense of God's word you have to compare one piece to another, which will use your time. Yet, each piece gives you a clue that will add to what you know and help you to explain, what God is telling you. When you fit one piece into another piece you begin to see more of an idea that God's word is pointing to. When each piece a clue to the puzzle is put in place in your mind a picture to look at.

You can change God's word when you to add to his word or take some of them out. When God speaks he is frank so, "Do not go beyond what is written." 1 Cor 4:6. You can assume too much and give God credit for ideas that are not in his word. That may put you in conflict with God, so confirm what you think God said. On the other hand, letting air out of the tire is what you do when you take from his word which makes you work with something that doesn't work for you. To have success, you must use the entire plan of God but how you interpret God's word changes the outcome of your life.

Start from scratch, check the doctrines you heard at church by the words they used. When you do not find those words in the Bible, the teaching may not be right. Comparing what you have against the word of God is the only way to find the truth. The study of God takes time but tells you what he will do or will not do. God's word is the truth and will not vary from what he does. You will find that God states his ideals more than once and it is consistent with what you know as true.

Pray

If you make no other rule to study God's word with, make this rule the first. Talk to the author who inspired the Bible before you get into God's word. Prayer is a good way to start whether you read or study. Tell God what you need from your time and ask God to explain his word to you. God will talk to you as you study for he will guide you into the truth, now its your turn to listen for his gentle voice.

Keep what he says in mind and do your best so you may rightly divide his word. Asking God for help is one way to get God involved. Truth is truth, but when God tells you the truth you will remember it the rest of your life. So ask God to pour his heart to you or reveal Christ in you. Then open your mind to the ideas you hear for it may be God making his thoughts known to you. Remember to trust in God for he has promised to give you the truth without finding fault in why you asked. (paraphrased James 1:3.)

Make a plan that fits your needs.

Plans take time and chance out of your life and make your goals happen. Plans give you a feasible way to make God's words yours to cherish. God has offered you a plan of Salvation to show the way to heaven. God told Joshua that by doing all that is written in the law that he would have success. By doing all that is in his word you will have the success of knowing God for yourself. Going to heaven should not be your primary goal as eternal life is found in knowing God. So make a plan to know God who would love to help you make that goal real by his desire to know you.

As you study God's word you will see the expertise of God in handling his life. You will see why God lives the way he does. It is hard to find fault with those that live the way you do, therefore how can God find fault with you if you live as he does? God has a reason to behave in a holy manner for it benefits those he associates with.

Is knowing God worth the trouble if you try but stop studying? You may lose interest in study if it does not fit your needs so modify the plans to fit your needs. Everyone under the sun have a plan for you to study God's word. They may have ideas that help you to make a plan to study so try a few of their ideas to see if they have the right way for you.

Bear in mind, not all people think alike for only a few lead neat and orderly lives. Some plan all the work that they do and some fly by the seat of their pants. The plan they offer may not be what you can use but you can glean from their ideas and let them serve as a guide to show you how to study. Set a goal for a study plan to fit your needs and one that will keep you in God's word.

Make God's word a part of your daily life.

The purpose of study is to know God's word so when you do it you will have success. God said do not let the book of law depart from your mouth. God's will is for you to keep a constant flow of his word going into your spirit. It leads you to a stable life like the rock of Christ, whose word will stand forever. This one rule will stabilize your life so that when the storms of life come, your house will not fall in ruins. Make it a law that you will read his word daily to know God.

God does not change.

Habits are hard to change and like man, God has habits. God's has a plan that rules the habits he uses to guide his life. God's word is like a rock that time and the storms of life have little affect on. His word will stand forever and it does not change. God has a stable life and his word gives you a sound pattern to live by. God's word is consistent as his outlook on life, thus you can build your life on the solid foundation of his word. The sun rises and sets every day and your study plan should be as consistent as the sun. God made his ways clear to man that, "I the LORD do not change." Mal. 3:6.

God is frank.

God is known to be all-powerful being and strong in every area of his life. One of those areas is in expressing his needs to those he rules and loves. God does not imply what he wants you to know or do. God is frank in his speech and his words are clear on the ideals he speaks about. God is not impartial for he says the same things to all men. God is not out to hurt your feelings or step on your toes but his words do not contain any ifs, and, or buts so you won't have any excuses. God is frank to every one because he wants you to know the right way to live. You can not argue with God when he speaks, for when God is done talking there is no dispute over what he wants you to do.

God's word agrees with his Character.

God shares his life, his ways and his ideals with you. He goes out of his way to treat you with respect, first he forgives you then sheds his grace on you. God's character is one way to test your beliefs and the things that God teaches you to do. He has not held anything back that you need to know or do.

You can tell when some of the things said about God do not sound like what he would do. You know what God is like and the way he talks just by spending time with him. You know God does not imply or beat around the bush but the time you have spent with God has made you sure of what he stands for. The hunch or the way you feel, tells you that something is wrong which will drive you into his word to know where the error is.

Truth is a principle.

Truth plays a big role in your life for it is the basis of trust in any relationship. This is why God asks that you worship him in spirit and truth. God does not lie but if you lie, where does the trust others have in you go? God has more reason not to lie than you do and that is the reason why you can trust his word. Jesus said, "If you hold to my teaching, you are really my disciples." Then you will know the truth, and the truth will set you free." John 8:31-32. Truth gives you the power to live for it is the facts you know to be true that keeps you safe.

> Every matter must be established by the testimony of two or three witnesses.
>
> 2 Cor. 13:1.

Paul gave you a way to prove the truth of the Bible. Facts do not change and when facts from two sources agree, you have a truth that you can rely on. When facts agree they show you a consistent pattern that you can trust. God's word is the truth and the gauge that sets you free when you find it. Be sure you find the truth of God's word when you study so you may serve him in truth.

Truth has an alarm that goes off when the lies are mixed with facts you know are true. The lie is the fact that did not agree with what you knew to be true. It's when your son Tom said he was over at Bill's house all day. Tom did not know that you had talked that day to Bill's dad in his garage, in addition, Bill's dad said that he hadn't seen Tom all day. You know you did not see Tom in the time that you were there. Tell me if you can, how did you know Tom was lying?

The facts did not jibe with what you knew to be true and you knew that Tom's story was not true. To know the truth, you will ask Tom questions until you get to the truth. Tom will cling to his story until he knows that you know the truth.

There will be no peace until you have the truth from Tom. As a result, the lie kept Tom in a trap until the truth comes out.

Tom's lie is the soldier who is out of step with his unit and he's not hard to find. He will be the one who is not in harmony with the rest of his squad. When marching, he will be up in the air when the rest are down. He will lean to the right when the rest are leaning to the left. He simply does not conform to the unit's cadence. On the other hand, your life has to conform to commands of God so he will see Christ in you.

God's words tell stories you can relate to.

Men see ideas in picture form so I asked God to show me how to explain this point. That night, my wife and I went out to eat where I saw a print of a "Norman Rockwell" on the wall. Like all of his work, the content said it all. What I saw were three boys that were running as fast as they could. Each boy varied in stages of dress and was looking as if they had been caught in the act. In the background was a sign "No Swimming Allowed." That told the story and without it the painting would not have made sense. There was no need to show those chasing the boys or the pond behind the weeds. It gave insight to the fear on their faces, and why they were in such a hurry. I recalled my youth when I used to swim in a like place and did the same things.

God's word tells stories in a way that you can see the same things in your life. Look closely at what the men of God did as the same kind of men live today. God used men like you to do great acts of valor and even they cried out to God when the trial came on them. You can learn from the kind of life these men had for God will help you as he did for them. These stories help you to know God since his word is the truth and then you can rely on the grace of God.

God wants you to love him and his way of life helps you to love others. God wants you to treat men the way that you want to be loved. The Bible tells the truth even when the deeds of men are not what God wants. The Bible will not tell you what to do but the story makes you the judge of what you need to do. God lets you see events that you may face in life so when the trials of life come, you will know what to do. The world tells you that no one will look out for you but God teaches that he will help when you look out for his needs.

How the words are used.

One word can affect how you use them as words show you a picture of what was said. The word bow is used in many ways but does the word bow agree with your picture? A bow can be on a gift, in a girl's hair or the front end of a boat. It is the right way to greet a King and a weapon used to shoot arrows. It is also an arc in the sky after it rains and the tool drawn across the strings of a violin. Bow is spelled one way and can be pronounced two ways but a bow is a thing that curves. The way bow is used tells you which one it is.

Words can go to the extreme opposites but they help you to know God's way of thinking. Good and evil and black and white are good examples. Black soaks in all the rays of the color range while white reflects all the rays of the color scale. Antonyms give you a way to see a truth as in this case black hoards color and white reflects. Black is to evil as white is to good and with words like this God can show good from evil, life from death, and right from wrong. God uses these words to clue you in and to show you that there is no gray area to God. You are one or the other.

When you have gone as far as you can with a word, look to see how the word was rendered. Men use other words to show the same idea as if wine was the blood of the grape. Take a look at how the word is defined or how that word is used in God's word.

Key words set the tone of the subject and help you to define the way the writer made his point. Often key words reflect the change of the writer's thoughts or to show how the ideas differ, are the same or show you the same idea in another form. Key words give you a way to sort the ideas, to compare and shape the truth of God's word. You may say that key words keep you on the same page with the writer. Most key words are adverbs that can be used as conjunctions or start a sentence. Below are some key words that help you see the ideas that the prophets wanted you to see.

A.) Therefore and for, are key words that tell what you are about to read is the why you can do what you just read. They are key words that tell you to go back and see why they are there that show a relationship to the idea as a whole.

B.) Because, for and for this reason, are words that show why the event took place or why you can or can't do it. These words explain that there is a reason that you need to be aware of that have a relationship to a previous idea.

C.) However, but and except are words that says something does not conform to the rule. It is a way to contrast ideas or to say how one idea differs from another.

D.) As, so and like are words that link two ideas to show that how they are similar.

Ask the Right Question.

Scientist study to know the secrets of life but his skill relies on the questions he asks. The answer lets him know more about what occurred, how did it change or how did it react to other things. Questions come from the need to know and for ideas that solve your need. How, where, when, what, why, and who are words that start the question for any study. They aim for one fact of the topic and make those facts stand out.

Keep Notes.

Keeping notes is like putting hay in the barn, so you will have hay all year long. Write your ideas down on paper so you have notes when you need them. Notes start you off where you stopped and serve as a way to go over your work. You can lose ideas that you do not put on paper so make notes on what you have done. Keeping notes will help you to fix what you learn in your mind. God keeps notes as well, your name is in the Book of Life to remind God of what you have done. (Refer to Mal. 3:16.)

CHAPTER 7

Learning To Think In A Godly Fashion

That you may meditate day and night. Joshua 1:8 Climbing a mountain is easy when you never go near one but your idea of it changes when you stand at its foot. The mountain dares you to climb it as the road only goes so far, and then it is by foot. Your life relies on what you take with you and you tire sooner when you are near the top for it's harder to breathe. The effort to reach the peak tests your skills so much that when you reach the top, all you can do is flop. Then, suddenly it hits you, Wow! Isn't that view just spectacular.

Wow! Is God talented or what. The view of his work has changed how you see God and there at the top you can't help but know that God exists. You come away knowing that God made the mountain and all you can see. Because of your size, you may wonder how and where you fit in God's plan. Why would God want to know me when his creation is so huge?

God wants you to have a long and prosperous life but to achieve that goal God wants you to think about his word day and night. Up to this point of God's plan all he wanted you to do was to put the book of law in your mouth. Now he wants you to chew on his word for the power to apply his word to each task of your life. Your father wants you to do everything the way he tells you to do them. David wrote. "Taste and see that the LORD is good." PS 34:8. The wisdom of God has the power to change your life but you have to try his word out to see if his ideals work. You will soon find out that the truth will change how you think and act since his word works in favor for your life.

Man uses his knowledge not only to earn a living but also to live with others. God cares how you think and he knows that the kind of food your spirit eats is crucial to the way you live. "You do not live on bread alone but on every word that comes from the mouth of the God." Deut 8:3. Bread is as much a need for the flesh as God's word is to your spirit. So you need to eat, chew and digest both kinds of food to live. Science may give you the way to earn a living but God's word gives you the power to live. God has given you the skills to live a holy life but you are the only one that can use those skills to be holy. God's word is a place of refuge but it is also a way to live.

Why meditate?

By watching daytime TV talk shows you may ask how depraved can people be? It all comes down to one thing and that is the way men think. Your mind is the part of you that thinks, manages your flesh and controls what it says and does. The people that make you sick to your stomach not only think what they have done is right but that you had it coming. The truth is that you will do what you think is right and will fight tooth and nail to defend your ways. What grieved God was the thoughts and intents of men were evil all the time (Gen 6:5) which made it easier to do evil. God knows that you have to think out your life and you need a plan to shun evil.

God has a reason for you to keep his law in your mind, as it gives you a plan to live by. The way people do things change the way you think and the way you think affects the way you do things. For a holy life you need a code of ethics that you can only find in the word of God. The word of God reflects the character of God and knowing his word will help you to know God. Knowing the plan God has for all men is to know what God expects of you.

God's word says. "My son, if you accept my words and store up my commands within you, turning your ear to wisdom and applying your heart to understanding, and if you call out for insight and cry aloud for understanding, and if you look for it as for silver and search for it as for hidden treasure, then you will understand the fear of the LORD and find the knowledge of God. For the Lord gives wisdom, and from his mouth come knowledge and understanding." Prov 2:1-6.

God has told you the kind of life that he wants you to have. To know and agree with the kind of life God has for you is to know that God has your needs in mind. By meditating day and night in his word you will know God and begin to think the way he does. Think of it this way, armed with the mind of Christ you can live a holy life pleasing to God. By thinking as God does, you will know what to do when the storms of life strike you. When you face the trials of life with God at your side you will come out smelling like a rose.

How to keep his word in your mind?

As a child, you were taught the ABC's and began to read and write. A cue card was held up for you to see and then you were asked to tell the teacher what it was. Your class would recite all the letters until the class had it right and then you sang the ABC's one more time. Each of these ways taught you the ABC's and it is part of how you think and live now. Time is the proof that this plan has worked and they will use this plan for your grand kids in the years to come.

A new job comes with a raise but you need to learn the new job. In a few weeks you can do that job in your sleep and you got the job down pat while doing it. You learned the ABC's the same way by doing the same steps again and again. You may think that you can't learn God's word, word for word but you can with the right motive.

How do you make the armor of God a part of your life until you take up the sword of the spirit? Grab it by force or to seize God's armor as your possession is what Paul meant when he said take up the sword. God gave his word to all men and he wants you to use it for his glory. The work you do to put God's word in your mind and makes God's work second nature to you. You will have a skill to use God's word any place God sends you.

How many times did you go over the steps before you got the ABCs and your job in your mind? You pick up the ABCs a few letters at a time and then go on to the next one. You spoke them, wrote them, or did them ten times a day or more. Use as many ways to learn as you can but do what it takes to have God's word in you. You did this as a child and there is a good chance that you can still sing the ABC song to the tune.

What do I gain by meditating?

Don't people pencil in the date and time in a book to know where they need to be? For some, it's in black and white to remind them but others keep these facts in their mind. Their day is planned out so that they will not miss the event they need to be at. A notebook is good for one goal but God has a plan for your life. You don't know when things will occur to change your life and you may not have the time to look things up. A sure thing is that sin can ruin your life in a split second but takes a long time to regain the life you had.

Your mind is a non-stop thinking machine that you need to keep well oiled. God made your mind like an audio tape because it came blank and you can put any idea in it and record over what's there. You direct your life as you see fit but you create the problems of life as well as solve them in your mind. You have to train your mind how to think or the world will do it for you. When the world trains your mind to think you end up doing the things that you don't want done to you. However, you can be God like when you let God teach you how to think. God wants you to spend your time thinking on the principles that tell you how to live. Perhaps, God wants you to take life seriously. On the other hand God doesn't want you to perish but give you life with hope and a future.

Forsakes your old ways.

Until the day that you found out what God plan was and what he has done for you, you lived as you saw fit. You took things and lied to make yourself look better. You scoffed at those who tried to tell you the good news and wanted nothing to do with God. When you met Jesus face to face, your life as you knew it had changed and you saw for the first time the kind of life you had been living. It was on that day that you knew that you had to change and with God's help you would change.

God's word gives you a way to change your

thinking. "Therefore, get rid of all moral filth and the evil that is so prevalent and humbly accept the word planted in you, which can save you." James 1:21. Forsaking your old ways meant changing habits that you owned for years. You found that there were more bad habits than lying and stealing to contend with but that sin had filled your speech as well. Giving up your old ways is hard to do even when you want to please God, but the effort you make to graph God's word into your soul is able to save you.

Builds a trust in God.

Time with God tells you that God does not have a plan to harm you. Your opinions of God changes when he comes through for you every time you ask for help. God is love and you are more apt to do his will as you begin to know and love him. God affects your life by keeping his word to you and you start to lean on him as a friend. The time that you spend with him will help you to see that God wants what is best for you. God knows how to build trust and he will teach you how to build trust with men.

Stabilizes your life.

People change with the problems they face but God does not change how he lives. God speaks of the double minded man who is unstable in all his ways. God gives you his word to stand on because his word does not waver or change with the wind. When you obey his word you stand on the foundation of God's word. The result is that you give God the proof he needs so God knows what you stand for.

Jesus spoke of the man who built his house on the sand and when the storms of life came on his house it fell. God's word is a rock for your life that comes with a promise that each word will not return to him void. You can trust God to watch over his word to see that it's done according to his will. The need to build your life on the rock of God's word is your life. Because it does not change, you will be able to stand against the storm. God will know where you stand and will be ready to help you.

Purifies your mind.

God is pure so you need to be pure but it only takes one thought to ruin your life. The value of a car is ruined by a dent and a blot will make a gem lose its value. Your thoughts lead to deeds so you need to rule over your thoughts. God demands the best you can give him and a life without sin keeps you fit for God's use. You have to keep the things that go through your mind in check to rule your life. Fill your mind with his word and think on things that lead to a holy life.

"But each one is tempted when, by his own evil desire, he is dragged away and enticed. Then, after desire has conceived, it gives birth to sin; and sin, when it is full- grown, gives birth to death."

James 1:14-15. Your thoughts can get between you and the God whom you serve with all of your heart and all your soul. Your mind can give birth to the desires of sin for sin is conceived in your mind. Sin is best stopped while it is still a thought because the longer you think on evil things, the more apt you are do them. By contrasting God's word with your thoughts you can see your thoughts as being wrong. God's word will keep your thoughts in check to keep you out of sin but when you sin, you cross the line. Keeping your mind in check with God's word will help you to serve God with your entire mind, heart, and soul.

Keeps your mind on the Job.

Employers stress that you need to keep your mind on the job because too many products leave the assembly lines incomplete. The goal is clear, since it is the three-cent part makes his product work. It cost your employer more to go back and fix the part than its worth. Money is not a concern of God for when you obey God you are the product God wants. God's word is the three cent part that makes your life as a Christian work.

God asks you to meditate day and night to be careful to do all that is written in his plan. God will not tell you to wake up, keep your mind on the job, or do your job right. Each part of God's plan is critical to your life but you have to do all of it for God's plan to work. If any part of the plan is left out God's plan will not work, as it should.

Meditation helps you to see right from wrong.

Men abuse the truth of God's word so that all you see is the sin that they get away with. Their deeds can make you think that if they can get away with sin so can you. The world you see runs in frenzy, without a goal for a holy life. God gave you his word to know right from wrong and that you may have a future free of harm. When you obey God you will never have to look back to know whether what you have done is right or wrong. God demands that you weigh your thoughts to act properly to stop sin in its tracks.

Meditating tells you how and why you need to live by God's principles. However, the world sees you as out of place and as something different when you live a godly life. Your friends will see the way you live and look at you closer. You make life better for others and in return you will be respected for the way you live. You should know that your life is the only Bible that others may see and they may want to have the life you have.

The goal is a changed life.

Sin starts as a thought in your mind but thinking on it gives birth to sin. On the other hand, your thought life helps you to have the life God wants you to have. God's word is the seed of your thought life and when you take time to dwell in it will yield the will of God in your life. God wants you to have a holy life, but you must limit your thoughts to what is holy and pure.

CHAPTER 8

What Is Success In Life?

> That you may be careful to do everything written in it. Then you will be prosperous and successful.
>
> Joshua 1:8.

Life can be dull if you do little to improve your life but it calls for work on your part. Life has its rewards but to thrive in life you have to make the effort to live. God wants you to excel with the tools he gave you and if for no other reason you can be a dynamic person like he is. You have the potential to be like God but your part is to hone the skills he gave you. Success is a choice when you to do your part and make the effort to live the way God wants you to live.

People have always thought that you have to be rich to be prosperous. Wow! Is there anything new under the sun? For most, the goal is to have a lot of money and all the things that make a life easy. They may spend their time at parties to have fun but the truth is that most of the rich have more dollars than sense. To keep their good life they hoard what they have but are they happy or do they have peace of mind without God?

Most people work so that they can have a life of luxury. They get up with the chickens and go to bed with the cows to have the things this world offers. The world as a whole thinks the person who dies with the most toys was a success in life. Who are you kidding, will those things follow you into the next life. God will burn the toys that you played with but the fruit of the spirit, God gave you, can go with you.

Life is a choice and it makes sense to seek a life that does not end. Success in life leads to an excess of life that God will give you. Listen to what God says. "For God so loved the world that he gave his one and only Son, that whoever believes in him shall not perish but have eternal life. John 3:16. Now this is eternal life: that they may know you, the only true God, and Jesus Christ, whom you have sent." John 17:3. Be wise in how you think for life does not consist of what you have but in whom you know and trust.

Success is a plan?

It's not likely that you would go to school and not put what you know to work. Let's say a man went to School and became a doctor. He had a license to practice but took a job as a farm hand making less than a doctor would earn. His heart was in being a farmer and later in life he bought a farm of his own. He had healthy animals but he did not use the skills he got from school on men. Would you go to him if you were sick?

It may seem absurd for you to know what God demand of you, but not do your part of his plan is just as absurd. That is what people do when they know God's word but do little to put God's word to use. The Lord desires that you use his word so success and obeying God goes hand in hand. "Do not merely listen to the word, and so deceive yourselves. Do what it says." James 1:22. Give God's word some thought for his word is his will for your life. Step out in faith knowing that God has promised that you would have success by doing all that is written in his word.

God has given his child his word, the mind to reason, and a way to apply his word in his day to day life. God has a plan for you to use, "A plan to prosper you not to harm you, a plan to give you hope and a future." Jer 29:11. Have you noticed God's rank and the universe he owns? God got all the things you can see by this plan and then he gave you his plan to live by. When you use God's plan, you will respect who he is and will admire the way he lives.

You work hard just to beat out a living but most of the time there is not enough time or money to go around. If you had dreams they went up in smoke and then you wonder if your life was worth the effort. All there is, is work and little of what you think success in life is, so you got a side job. That gave you the money to buy the stuff your family needed but stole what to your family needed the most, your time and love. You can be so busy working for your needs that you forget those you love and why you have those goals. All that means is that you can focus on one part of your life and let the important things in life pass by.

What is God's Part?

When you read and study God's word, you will see that your father in heaven wants what's best for you. Like your father on earth God has the duty to show his child how to make the right choices in life. God wants you to do what is right, just and fair to your peers. God gave you the choice to know how he wants you to live and has a plan to ensure your success in life.

Find out what God demands then do a trial run to see if it works. To find out just how good God is you need to see if God responds to your need. Was your answer exactly what you needed, if so then will you try other things God wants you to do? God has to keep his word to you since you will not trust him if he does not. You will never know how good God can be unless you put his word to use in day to day life. Applying God's word is your part to trust God but will you trust him with your life if he does not keep his word?

God has a specific number of men he has planned for (Rev. 6:11). God does not want the world to perish

(John 3:16, 2 Peter3:9). God is in you to help you as you take each step (John 14:23). God has said that his word will do what he sent it to do (Isa.55:11). He has promised to give you the things you ask of him (John 14:13). God watches over his promises to see that they are kept (Jer. 1:12). All this shows that God goes the extra mile to work his plans, and no one can thwart his plans (Isa 14: 24-27).

The best part of God's plan is when he comes to live in you to help you. Christ said. You may ask me for anything in my name, and I will do it. "If you love me, you will obey what I command. "And I will ask the Father, and he will give you another Counselor to be with you forever." John 14:13-16. "When he, the Spirit of truth, comes, he will guide you into all truth. He will not speak on his own; he will speak only what he hears, and he will tell you what is yet to come. He will bring glory to me by taking from what is mine and making it known to you. All that belongs to the Father is mine. That is why I said the Spirit will take from what is mine and make it known to you." John 16:13-15.

> "Therefore, my dear friends, as you have always obeyed— not only in my presence, but now much more in my absence— continue to work out your salvation with fear and trembling, for it is God who works in you to will and to act according to his good purpose."
>
> Phil 2:12-13.

God is going to do every thing in his power to give you success. Through his word God gives you the desire to do his will and then he will work with you to do his will. The problem is that man falls short of doing God's will because they do not lean on God for the right answers. Men rob God of his glory when they try to do God's will in their power.

God wants you to meditate so you can do all that is written in the book of the law. For it is by working God's plan in entirety that you will succeed in the life God wants you to have. God's promises makes a way for you to be sure that you will succeed. However, you make God's choice sure when you do the things God has planned for you to do. God did not plan for you to fail for he is letting you have his secrets to give you a way to succeed. All you have to do is apply his word to your life.

What is life to success in life?

What is success in life if you measure it by the world standards? First you must establish what life is and what makes life worth living. Life is the time between birth and the present but life in this world ends. God gives life to those who seek his gift so that the idea of what success in your life should change with it. God wants to give you a life that has no end but you need to think of life in the same way God does.

All you have to do is look at God to see what success in life is. God may not know how old he is but what he does know is how to succeed. He does not burn the bridges behind him as men do for he may need them later on. He has learned what to do the first go around so he does not have to come back to fix what he has done wrong. God knows that what he does affects his life and he lives in such a way that he can look forward to what life brings. Success in life lets you have an abundance of life to share with others. The gift of life God wants to give you is his way to share the excess of life he has with you.

The plan God has given to you in Joshua 1: 8 is a plan to know and love God. To this end, God wants you to spend time with him to learn how to prosper. The effort you make to do all that is written in God's word will help you to thrive in every area of your life. God gave you a plan to achieve life but you have to do your part to succeed.

PART TWO

Going in God's Strength

God is a dynamic being with a plan for you to succeed. You probably have heard the saying like father, like son so you should reflect the choices your father makes. When you spend time with your father, he will show you how to excel. God has given you a command to be strong but you may not know how to be strong in the Lord. In the chapters ahead you will learn what being strong in the Lord means.

I used this definition for the word "Strong." from the Fourth Edition, of the American Heritage Dictionary of the English Language 2000, which may help you to understand what being Strong in the Lord means;

1. Physically powerful; capable of exerting great physical force.
2. In good or sound health; robust.
3. Economically or financially sound or thriving.
4. Having force of character, will, morality, or intelligence.
5. Having or showing ability or achievement in a specified field.
6. Capable of the effective exercise of authority.
7. Capable of withstanding force or wear; solid, tough, or firm.
8. Having great binding strength.
9. Not easily captured or defeated.
10. Not easily upset; resistant to harmful or unpleasant influences.
11. Having force or rapidity of motion.
12. Persuasive, effective, and cogent. Extreme; drastic.
13. Having force of conviction or feeling; uncompromising.
14. Intense in degree or quality.

These 14 qualities define the strengths of God. However, God is the origin of all strength, thus you must look to God for his strength. These definitions reflect the strength the character God wants you to have and the quality of life depicted in God's word in harmony with the spiritual principles of God. The chapters that follow depict the strengths God uses to be the Almighty God that is worshipped by the body of Christ. After reading the following chapters you will see why you need to apply these strengths to the work you do for God.

CHAPTER 9

Giving A 110%

Today, Christians have no clue of what it means to be strong in the Lord. It's not that the church does not teach how to be strong but they do not link its teaching to being strong. God shows you how to use the sum of your spirit to rule your life and avoid evil. As your coach would do, God asks that you use 110% of all that you have to run the race and more so when you clash with Satan. That may not be as easy as you may think, for Satan uses 110% of his skills to make you believe his lie. You need to arm your mind with the mind of Christ to be armed with the truth.

How do you resist Satan who has had ages to refine his skills as a liar to an art? Satan has been there, seen it, and done it and knows how to set his trap. He will use his skills to tempt you in every way he can but you must submit to God. Satan will keep you under his thumb until you yield your life to God and obey his word. God wants to set you free of sin but you have to do your part to resist sin.

You need the tools that do the job and not fall apart before the job is done. Tools come in sizes, some will do the job and others will not. The 1\2 hp saw cuts all right but it will stall out when you push it too hard. You really have to push a 1hp saw to stall it out and it comes with features that allow you to do other jobs as well. In the same way, you don't have to drag, push or pull the truth for it has the power you need to run your life. In the race for your life, you need the strength to run hard so that you will not fall before you cross the finish line. God will teach you how to use the truth and help you to gain the skills you need in the race. Then he will be at your side with the help that you need when you need it.

> "Now to him who is able to do immeasurably more than all we ask or imagine, according to his power that is at work within us,"
>
> Ephesians 3:20.

It's not too hard for anyone to use the first part of this verse to ask for the things you want from God. However, it's just as important to allow God to work in you so you can use you for his glory. God is able to do more than you ask of him to do, but is limited by what you will let him do. You have the power of a living God in you but you have to let him show the world the power that is in you.

Your faith in God should direct your steps, but most Christians wait on God for signs of his power. That is not how God works, you have to take the first step.

Jesus chose to do the will of his father and ruled his life to do his will even when the cost was his life. He did all that he saw his father do and spoke the words he heard his father say. Then he went the extra mile, he gave all he had for the goal his father had. He went to the extreme for you and gave his all to make a way for you to know God. You also have the choice to rule your life in the same way and show the love God has for the world.

Intensity demands more of you.

Look back to the day when God came down to Mount Sinai to give his law to Moses. On that day the trumpet of God was so loud that you could not hear your thoughts. The ground trembled and rocks burst in the wake of God. The sights and sounds were such that those who heard and saw these sights thought they were going to die. God had man's attention and he gave them a reason to revere him.

The power of God is such that it can change you for the rest of your life. What was it that kept Saul from seeing with his eyes on the road to Damascus? Saul was told that he was fighting God and for three days and he had nothing to do but think about his life. What went through his mind in those three days changed the man that fought God to a servant of the good news. Was it the light or was it the power of God that changed Saul the Pharisee to Paul?

The people who ask you to do things for them do not want a poor effort. They want to know when the job will be done and if you have the time to do it. However, they also expect you to do your best. Your employer pays for your best and the team you play ball on wants you to give 110% to win. Your spouse wants all your love and your all is what your friends expect of you. Even God demands your best and wants to be first on your list. Giving your best to meet the needs of others is a good way to show others how you want to be loved.

Working on a team

Could you have done more or done it better when you work for God? Christ sent his disciples out in pairs so that they could help each other. Not only do they share the job but they also did not have as much to do per person. You may be able to do the job by yourself but it would be far easier and much faster with help. Doing any job with help is like adding more beef to the stew. The result is a more hearty stew with a taste that you will enjoy.

> "Two are better than one, because they have a good return for their work: If one falls down, his friend can help him up. But pity the man who falls and has no one to help him up! Also, if two lie down together, they will keep warm. But how can one keep

> warm alone? Though one may be overpowered, two can defend themselves. A cord of three strands is not quickly broken."
>
> Eccl 4:9-12.

When God created man the LORD God said, "It is not good for the man to be alone. I will make a helper suitable for him." Gen 2:18. God made man, male and female to be a unit. Why do you think God hates divorce? Life is hard to live alone but when two split up and go their own way and lose the strength of their mate. God gave you a mate to help you but he also gave you his spirit to make you stronger. Working as a team adds strength to the work that you do for God and makes you able to do more in the same time. God wants you to work in unity with him and show the world that God loves them and you now have Jesus to work with to help you spread the word.

The use of your skills.

Skill is gained by doing the same task hundreds of times. The skilled man can tell with his eyes shut where he's at and what the next step is. His work is second nature to him. You may feel that you are in the way when he is at work doing his job in front of you. His skills use his mind and body to function and those skills were not gained over night. Your skill means that you have an expertise to do a job no matter where you are and that skill gives you a way to command people. Once you learn the job inside out, people will come to you to do the job because you can get the job done. You will be able to advise them if it can be done and how it can be done.

It's a good thing that God gave each man a different skill but if every one had the same skill, how would you live? Skills give you a way to survive in the world, to one man God gave the gift to grow plants so you can have the food to eat. To another man the ability to drive a truck that brings the food to the store where you shop. Consider this, God gave you a skill not only to live but a skill for his glory. You face trials that will differ from other men and the trials will give you the skills that you will need in the future. You are more productive when you use the skills that God gave you wisely. Your skill is a gift that will work hand in hand with the work that God wants you to do.

Show God how you feel.

> "The tax collector stood at a distance. He would not even look up to heaven, but beat his breast and said, 'God, have mercy on me, a sinner."
>
> Luke 18:13.

You say more with your body than you say with your mouth. Look at the tax collector that stood at a distance refusing to lift his eyes, who beat on his chest. He said more with his body language than he did with his mouth. Can you hear the tone in this man's broken voice, isn't it full of anguish? God saw the pain this man was in and had to reach out to help him. Put yourself in God's shoes. Did you believe this man and were you willing to help anyway you could?

Did you know that you show God how you feel when you speak? Your face and the tone of voice will reflect how you feel. Anger is shown in one way and love in another. Your words can be mixed with tears when you cry out in pain to God. God will see your tears when you pray because you are in the throne room of God. God can feel your pain by the way you show your pain. Like the child who runs to you with a cut, you know that he is in pain by his crying, the look on his face and his clutch on the injury. That child used 110% of his feelings to make you believe how he was hurting. How long did it take for you to see the need to soothe his pain?

A good joke can make you laugh till your side aches and the joy that floods your eyes with tears. It's the truth of the joke that caused your joy and the ability to see the setting of the story as being so real to you and made you laugh hard. Are you real to God or are you putting on a show when you pray? You may want to ask God if he is just a fan of yours or is he the one who can answer your prayer. Just as you can see through others and know their motives God can see yours. Show God how you feel but show God the real side of you without pretenses.

Speak Boldly

How you convey your needs to others, is a concern that God has. When you pray, you need to be bold in speech yet humble in God's eyes. You can be bold and still give God the dignity he needs. What you say and how it is said helps to make the truth known when you go in to the throne room of God. You can speak clearly and give others the respect they need and say it in spirit and in truth.

Talk about the problem and leave the person at fault out of the debate. Be truthful, brief and to the point making the issue your main focus. Being blunt will leave no doubt of what you said and add force to the way you explain your ideas. For example: Peter and John were put on trial (Acts 4) for speaking in the name of Jesus. That night the church called on God, asking to speak the word of God boldly. Would you say that God said yes when the earth shook under Peter as he had prayed? Without saying a word God gave an answer when he shook the ground that they could not question.

God spoke boldly in his might and left no margin of error with his answer. God's reply gave these men the power to defy those who gave the order not to speak in the name of Jesus. Now they had no doubts that God was working with them.

God has a specific goal in mind and chooses the right words to do it. God is not afraid to say what is on his mind nor will he hold anything back on you. God wants you to be bold with your friends and tell the world where you stand. Tell the world that they need Christ by the way you walk the talk. Show the world that you love God, knowing that you do not have to lie or con anyone. You have a specific job to spread the gospel. God's word will stand on its own so be frank with the world and tell them the truth.

Teaming up for strength.

A rope with 1 strand will strain to lift an ounce but a rope with 100 strands will lift a ton. The point is that 100-strand rope will let you do more work than a single strand will do. God adds strands to your rope, which will let you do more than you can do alone. It's God desire to unite with you to give you the strength that you need to do his will but you also need him to satisfy your needs. God is greater than the one who is in the world and with God's help you can overcome the world. You are one strand of the rope and you could use God's strength to make it to the pearly gates.

God made man male and female with a demand to fill the earth. When God gives an order, he gives you a way that it can be done. Man has his part and the women hers to fill the earth with children but they have to unite. Clearly, God wants you to work as a team with others. The plan God chose to fill the earth has its reward and he gave you an incentive to agree with his plan.

In the Bible there is a story about the tower of Babel that you can learn how you can unite for strength. The men of this story were speaking in the same terms and chose to build a city with a tower. These men started with a goal to build a city and agreed that all would do their part to build the city. These men chose to unite to work as a team for the same goal and you could do the same with God? Did you hear what God had to say about these men? "Then nothing they plan to do will be impossible for them." Gen 11: 6. God wants you and the church to unite in one accord, then nothing would be impossible.

Two is the smallest unit that God asks man to work with so go in pairs and work as a team. Teamwork is a way that you can get more done and do it with strength. You can be strong and work side to side with God. God does his part in heaven and you do your part on earth. Then both of you will be pulling on the same rope, working for the same goal. You have to be one with God to be a part of the rope that you may go with God in his power.

Go the Extra Mile.

Do you ask God for your needs when he has the time or as soon as he can? Do you demand toys from God, but don't have the time for his needs. God has opened the door to his life but you can't enter his world on your terms. Would you let strangers in your home or those you know and can trust? God has taken the first step to know you by knocking on your heart's door but have you done anything to know him? Have you gone the extra mile to know him?

There need be no doubt in your mind that God wants you to go all out for him. You only have one shot to go to heaven so be prudent. Seek God first and love him with all your heart. As Jesus taught his disciples, "If someone forces you to go one mile, go with him two miles." Matt 5:41. Do all that is written in the book of the law and make every effort to live a godly life. "Whatever your hand finds to do, do it with all your might." Eccl. 9:10. "Therefore, my brothers, be all the more eager to make your calling and election sure. For if you do these things, you will never fall." 2 Pet. 1:10. God seems to go overboard to show you what he means by going the extra mile.

Going the extra mile is doing the job with all your might and completing the job in a godly manner. Do the best you know how to help others by using all your skills. As God's child you can call on God for help and know that God will go the extra mile for you. Doing what God expects makes it possible to exceed what you have been asked to do. You will cover all the bases when you have done all that is written in the book of law.

Your heart, mind, soul and strength make up who you are and all of these have to work as a unit. God's command is that you love God with all you have and he expects you to worship him in the same way. Just to raise your hand in the worship service takes your mind to order it, your might to lift your hand, and your heart to say you want God to see your hand. All is the extent that God counts on and when you give all, you get God's best.

CHAPTER 10

Confronting Life, When It Doesn't Go Right

My wife makes up classes to train the people her company employs. She gets a list of names and then she sends a letter to notify them of the time and place of the class. Sounds simple but do you know that after they get the letter they call her for the details? She asks them if they got a letter but they still want to know what it's all about. She asks them to read the part of the letter that she sent them to answer the question they have. Some just want to know what they have to do rather than read the letter she sent. That baffles her to no end and makes her ask what else could she have done to do her job.

God did the same with the Bible for he has put all you need to know in his word. God then used men to write what you need to know into a book so you could read it. With his letter, God knows that you do not have an excuse to know what he wants from you. God went out of his way, to let you know what he wants from you but the question is, will you use your brain to find what God wants from you. Is it easier to ask the men of God what to do, than it is to read the letter God sent to you?

Why do you think God would go to all the trouble to put his word in a book? The primary reason is that God's word and the printed word does not change over night as men do. The world has its own ideas that tell you how to live and it does not agree with what God wants. God gave you his word so you can have the straight scoop and a source of pure truth to refer to when you need it. God knows that life is a series of choices that you make but he is not going to force you to obey him. The truth of God's word puts you in the driver's seat and that gives you the right to choose the way you live. Right or wrong on the day you stand before God, you can say that you were in control of your life.

You can do things your way or you can do things God's way. You are in opposition with God when you assume to know more than God does. As a result you do things your way and do not follow his plan or ask others how to do the job. The choice is in your hands but it's your life that is at stake too. Doing things your way when you work for others does not work for they have reasons to want things done their way. People see the faults in your life just as you find fault in the way they do things but they do not go out of their way to tell you that the way you live offends them. You offend God with your arrogance when you assume that God will do things for you the way you want it done. When that happens, God will go on with his life letting you deal with your own problems.

God will confront you.

God has loved you from the day God made you but he has made you responsible for your deeds. God loves you so much that he will confront the way you live in the same fashion that he has in the past. To Adam, God said, Who said you are naked? To Cain, where is you brother and to Saul, what is this bleating in my ears? God knew the answer to these questions but he asked to let you know that he knew. Why would God confront the way you live? God loves you so much that he does not want you to be one of the weeds that he is going to burn on the day he comes for his people.

In John's vision of Christ, he repeats what Christ said. "To the church, Christ said, I hold this against you" Rev 2:4, "I have a few things against you" Rev 2:14, And again "I know your deeds." Rev 2:19. God is telling you these things today, not so much to let you know that he knows but to let you consider what you are doing. God's idea is to wake you up and show that you need to do something to be right with him. You can't read God's mind but you can thank God for telling you that you are in sin. You need to know how God feels so you can change what you're doing which makes your relationship to God even stronger.

The desire to share your life with others makes life better. Being close to anyone and sharing your life with others, will force them to see the faults you have. Who needs your faults when your faults offend those who see them? To make life better, your faults have to be brought out to the open so you can see what you are doing to hurt others. You need to tell your friend why this fault offends you and how you feel so that their dignity stays intact. When done right, no one else needs to know and you will have your friend for life.

God loves you but your sin keeps you apart from God. When God says that you have sinned, God really wants you to make things right with him to stay on friendly terms. Sin offends God and when he comes to tell you that what you have done is wrong, you need to make things right. God will tell you what he sees as a sin and gives you the dignity to tell your side of the story or say that you were wrong. God is also saying that sin offends his sense of right and wrong and that sin is not fair to anyone as well as you.

The proof is in the royal laws that God is a God of relationships. God loves you and wants to be at your side as long as you live. Sin is the issue that you have to face to be right with God. "Come now, let us reason together," says the LORD. "Though your sins are like scarlet, they shall be as white as snow; though they are red as crimson, they shall be like wool. If you are willing and obedient, you will eat the best from the land; but if you resist and rebel, you will be devoured by the sword." For the mouth of the LORD has spoken." Isa 1:18-20. Sin destroys your relation with God and by reasoning together you have a way to keep your life on the up and up with God.

What happens when you ignore God?

Have you had a crush on someone and tried to introduce yourself to him or her? You wink at them and go to them to talk but they look past you as if you weren't there. You came close to shouting, look I am in front of you, why won't you talk to me? Then, you know they saw you but they snub you and turn away. That has to be how God feels when the world knows that he lives but chooses to avoid him. Being snubbed or rejected by anyone is hard to bear. It hurts when you have gone out of your way to show your love for them and they still turn away from you. A time comes when you say enough, is enough. Go your own way. See if I will ever want, need or help you.

God loves you so much that he will let you have your hearts desire (Ps 37:4). Sounds strange when you want nothing to do with God but he will still give you, your heart's desire. God made hell for those who want to live their own way and want nothing to do with God. However, there is nothing so bad that God can't forgive and to make your life right with God. God has confronted you with a choice of life or death and he has given you the right to choose the one you prefer.

Confronting man's weakness.

The Lord your God is an almighty God who gave you "Ears that hear and eyes that see, the Lord has made them both." Prov. 20:12. God expects you to open your eyes and ears to him for his strength. If you will listen to God and obey him, he will show you how to be strong.

Most men think that God wants to rule your life with an iron fist and balks at the idea but to the contrary, God wants you to rule your life. The world has turned its eyes and ears turned off to God they do not seek life in the spiritual realms. Consequently, the world runs from God even though God is motivated by love. God knows how to make good choices that do not come back to haunt you. God will work with you to help you make the right choices but he also gave you the time to learn how to rule your life.

On the other hand, Satan is a liar with a desire to rule your life any way he can. All he wants to do is to push you off to the side and keep you under his thumb. You are a pawn or a slave that will take the blame and the heat when you obey Satan. He will point his finger at you and cast the blame on you and instead of help he will laugh at you. Satan wants to rule your life without your consent for his use and his only.

The choice of life and death is in whom you listen to. Satan will not give you a choice, he will intimidate and lie to your face until you fall under his rule. To choose life you have to seek God of your free will and use all your might to serve him.

God wants you to choose life but Satan will do his best to keep you from the life God wants to give to you. You have to make the choice to seek God for Satan is going to do his best to make you sin.

Confronting your life.

"Why do you look at the speck of sawdust in your brother's eye and pay no attention to the plank in your own eye?" Luke 6:41. Why do condemn the sin of others and not see the sin in your life? God wants you to gather men into his flock yet how can you lead men to Christ when your sin is hung out to dry where the world can see it. God wants you to know how to deal with sin so that he can use you. To be in a position that you can lead men to Christ you first have to follow him yourself. That means you have to know what sin does and do what you know to do to get rid of it.

God said you could not pretend to be holy but you had to live a holy life. God does not want your life to be a fake for all to see but live in spirit and in truth for God. The good that comes out of your heart must be the fruit of the God's spirit and not the deeds of the world. Live your life so that Jesus is what others see and live in such a way that others will want what you have. You can not fake love for God so you have to train yourself to produce fruit that is holy to God your father.

"Sin crouches at your door; it desires to have you, but you must master it." Gen 4:7. You may not be of the world but the sin of the world can affect you because sin has a strong influence on you. You live in a world that sins and you can slip into the world by going with its flow. The world says that adultery is an affair and the murder of the unborn is the removal of fetal tissue. These words make it easy to agree to sin but to master sin you must be able to call a spade a spade. Sin is sin no matter how it is said. Sin is ready to rule your life but you must have a mind that is able to deal with sin. Those who shun evil live by God's word and know that the good inherits life but the wages of sin are death.

To be able to confront life you have to stand against the things that can ruin your life. Jesus spoke of the man that built his home on the rock would have a house that will not fall when the storms came. For you the storms that attack your life are the torrents of sin that strikes at your door. Sin is at your door but the wise man builds his life on the word of God and uses God's word as a plan to live by.

Confronting your Goliath.

Goliath influenced men in the time when David was in his teens. His size and skills made him a man that no one questioned and if they stood up to Goliath, they would pay with their life. Goliath used his size and brute strength to gain a place of respect but he was arrogant. Goliath used those attributes to show the world that sin was appropriate for the success of his job. Today you face that kind of evil in your life as people use their position or job to force their way of life on you.

David heard Goliath say to Israel that it was pointless to trust in God and since he trusted God, David was crushed to the soul. Imagine the thoughts that may go through your mind. Can you stand up to a man three times your size and would you be put to death or be hurt to oppose his views? With God's help, David chose to face Goliath who held Israel at bay and you too can face life with God's help. Use the influence you worked so hard to build to take a stand to resist evil.

You too have a Goliath to face and you need God's help to face him. You know the feeling that makes you stop and waver from what you are about to do. That feeling that stops you from telling your friend that God is good. Your feelings that tell you that something is wrong and makes you afraid of things you can't see, feel, or touch. It stops you at the moment you need, long enough for the right time to pass and that is time you will never see again. Those feelings can be the Goliath of your day that melts your heart.

What makes you afraid of making a move when you can't see what you are afraid of? That feeling always occurs when you are making a choice to do things that God wants you to do. It happens so much that the feeling stops you from telling the good news. The feelings that a muscle bound goon such as Goliath would give are not as true as you think. You are in the ranks of God's army just as much as Saul's men were. Waiting for Goliath to go away and do nothing to confront the evil in your life does not make sense. It did not take David long to see what the danger really was. He sought the heart of God and trusted God to confront his enemy.

Your need to confront.

Why is sin a big issue to God when sin is not an issue to Satan or his followers? Satan uses tactics similar to guerilla warfare where he strikes hard, does his damage and then runs for cover. Satan uses sin to steal, to kill, and destroy the kingdom that God is building. Satan is at war with God and sin is the loaded gun that kills men. Why would God love you and care about the way you live unless you were his child. Sin robs you of the respect you need as a human being for life. Sin ruins the work you have done and defeats the need to improve your life. Sin should be a big issue to you when you have to live with sin's penalty the rest of your life.

Confronting your life is your quality control department that keeps your life right with God. Successful people go over their plans to see where they are in relation with their goals. Scan over the fruit of your life to see if you have what God wants. If you see the fruits that God does not want, you have time to make changes. Fix the things that are wrong and do the things that Christians do to follow God's leading.

The final confrontation with sin.

"Woe to you who long for the day of the LORD! Why do you long for the day of the LORD? That day will be darkness, not light." Amos 5:18. As a Christian, you long for the day of the Lord for it is the day when your struggle with sin is over. What this verse tells you is that the day of the lord may not be what you expect. This will be the day when you pass under the rod of your Lord and receive your reward. No one knows exactly what will happen on that day but you can be sure that your sin will find you out.

The surprise will be to those who have made no effort to know God or to please him. "You will again see the distinction between the righteous and the wicked, between those who serve God and those who do not." Mal 3:18. "They will be punished with everlasting destruction and shut out from the presence of the Lord and from the majesty of his power on the day he comes to be glorified in his holy people and to be marveled at among all those who have believed." 2 Th 1:9-10.

CHAPTER 11

Your Influence And Being Persuasive

God gave you the right to decide how to run your life as you see fit. Since you are not an expert on life, you have to rely on other beings for help. The people nearest to you affect your choices and how they live determines whom you go to. You have to be careful to choose the right person for help because their advice can change the rest of your life. Knowing where to get help and the person that gives you advice has a value to you. The advice they give will be based on how they see life and you need a way to solve your problem that fits your way of life. Chances are that you will not go to anyone for help that you do not approve of the way they live?

Life is full of trials that force you to seek help but there is a parody in life. You may know the right way to do things but choose to ignore it. Paul said "what I do is not the good I want to do; no, the evil I do not want to do— this I keep on doing." Rom 7:19. Paul goes on to say, So I find this law at work: "When I want to do good, evil is right there with me." Rom 7:21. The parody is that you can sin when you know the right thing to do.

What compelled Paul to do the things he did not want to do? The Bible tells you that sin starts in the mind as a thought, then that thought leads to sin. The thoughts that enter your mind must be governed, especially when you get ideas from others. You may ask, where do the ideas that pop in your mind come from? That may sound strange but Satan advises what you should do whether you want it or not. Satan is one of those that sticks his nose into your affairs and tells you what to do. He is so sly that you will think that you came up with the idea. You need to know how you came up with the idea and what you base your reasons on. Satan is an expert at confusing you at the moment you make your decisions, causing you to hesitate long enough to revert to the ways of your old man. Thus you changed your mind even though you may have wanted to do the right thing.

Sources of Influence.

The way God, Satan, and your peers live can change the way you think. You may not want anything to do with God but where you go, the way others live, and Satan have the power to alter the choices you make. Some study the life of Caesar because he ruled the known world in his time and the influence that he had on the world in his lifetime. Yet only a few men study the life of Christ because he appears to have died a failure on the cross. In truth he subdued the world and gave you a way to have life, however, men are looking for a way to gain the world or a way to get more from life. Christ knew who he was and Caesar thought he was God but the main difference is that Christ is still alive today.

Men search for new ideas to use to make their lives better. Solomon said that there is nothing new under the sun but life has a habit of repeating it self. To find out what works, you may read books, ask God, and your friends. Yet you won't have to ask Satan for he will tell you what to do whether you want it or not. He's not going to tell you anything new or ask you to do things that will help you in the long run. God had his reasons to throw Satan out of his home and since his life did not suit God then, his ideas won't help you today either.

Trust, is Earned.

The people in your inner circle have your trust and you have learned to rely upon them for help. Those you trust are those that will influence you and it's from this circle that you seek help from. They have the power to change the way you think. Some people will never have your trust since the way they live tells you that their advice will give you the same trouble they have. They have no qualms to lie or take what they need or say one thing and do another. They may not mean to hurt you but they hurt you so much you wonder if their word is credible. Your opinion of them is based on how they treat you and the way they live.

Every day occurrences will change the way you think and the methods you use to have the things of the world. Those who desire the good life, seek the advice of those who have the kind of life they want. Wealth has a false sense of security and men have longed to be secure from the beginning of time. Wealth is like a fad that goes as fast as it comes and men want the problems that wealth brings. On the other hand those that have fame have things in their closet that they don't want you to see and they are not going to point them out. They distort the good parts of their life so you think of them in better light. Life is such that you can't trust your own eyes since people do things to impress you.

Do you protect your life from harm and guard the things you own from those you do not trust? Do you lock up your house when you are not at home so the things you own won't walk off? Will you loan your tools to anyone who brings your stuff back broken or you have to ask then to return them? Why do you drop those that lie to you from those you confide in? Those who have done these things have the trust they deserve but then trust is earned.

Satan's Influence.

His Origin.

Like men, Satan is a created being made to worship and serve God. Yet, God found sin in his life and dealt with Satan's sin. It was about this time that Satan rebelled, he wanted to rule heaven and have God's throne. In time, war broke out in heaven and Satan was thrown to the earth. Its plain to see that God won the war but Satan has not conceded the victory to God. He is filled with rage and is out to destroy the apple of God's eye.

The battle that you have as a Christian is not with men but with the evil that Satan brings on you. Your fight is with a being that you can not see or touch with your hands so you can't pick up a gun and scare this dude off. Even if you had the weapons that men use to fight wars, you would do no harm to him. Satan lives in the realm where God lives and you have to trust God to fight your battles for you.

The Bible is the source to know Satan and what he stands for. To some the idea that Satan exists is absurd partly because you tell your kids that the moon is made of blue cheese and the stork brought them hanging in a diaper. On the other hand you have no doubt that God made you and the earth that supports your life. God's word tells you that Satan is real so he can not be ignored. Why is that you say the devil made you do it but you don't want to admit that he can influence you? God gave you his word with a plan to resist the evil of the world but to resist evil, you must rule your life.

His plan.

Sin robs you of the right God gave to you to rule your life. Satan is the god of his own realm, but he is at war with God. You are a child of his enemy, making you a prime target to kill, steel, and destroy. Satan does not need you yet he wants to use you to hurt God. Should you fall into Satan's hands, you will be on your own for you are the spoils of this war. Satan wants you to fall from God's grace and when you sin you will become his slave. When confronted in a lie you will be a slave of the lie because you will lie again to make the lie look like the truth.

He Interferes.

Satan takes off his bells and whistles when he goes hunting or stalking his prey. You will be in his mouth and on the way to his den before you know he is near you. Satan is an expert at sneaking up on you, poking his nose in your affairs and giving advice that you don't need or want. Listen to his ideas and all you will want to do is sleep, eat, and be merry. His thoughts will stop you from doing what God wants you to do. When he is done with you, he will toss you into the fire with the rest of his motley bunch. However, if you submit to God, Satan will run for his life.

Satan uses your desires against you.

Men want to be on top when the smoke clears and gain the things of this world to boot. Satan knows that if you look long enough, you will find a way to have them. With that in mind, Satan gives you a easy way to reach your goals and uses your desires to put your morals on the shelf. Once he has your ear, he uses his skills to show you how to have you needs. The trap is set and when the smoke clears you are in the trap of guilt, because you believed his lies.

Satan is Persistent.

Satan is like that itch on your back that's just out of your reach when you go to scratch it. You can twist your arms into knots before you chase that itch over all your back. You may ask for help to scratch your back but all this does is to teach you how to give directions. Up a little, no, more to the left, lower. Ah! Finally! You got it. Only a minute later the itch is back to annoy you and Satan persists all the harder to keep you busy, scratching. You can't get rid of the itch or run Satan off for long. God is the only one that can help you, when you submit to God, that itch, like Satan will flee.

Influence that spirits impresses on man.

At times, man can base choices on his feelings but both God and Satan impress their needs on you.

God can stir you to take a step of faith and shun evil. Satan incites you to shy away from God's will and sin. The feeling of joy, love, guilt, and fear all come from the spirit realm and change the choices you make. To keep your feelings in check, sort those feeling's out to know whom they come from.

God's influence.

The Truth.

It is written, "For we cannot do anything against the truth, but only for the truth." 2 Corinthians 13: 8. To understand this verse you need to know that you can't fight truth because it is true. Truth is solid as a rock and won't budge an inch. The truth agrees with the things that are real and known to be true or factual. God seeks men that will worship him in spirit and in truth. To worship God in truth, you have to walk the talk and living by the spirit means that you follow God's leading. "Those who are led by the Spirit of God are sons of God." Rom 8:14 and "My sheep listen to my voice; I know them, and they follow me." John 10:27.

God said that you not only live by bread but by the word of his mouth. The word of God gives you one truth after another and the power to properly rule your life before God. When you study God's word "you will know the truth, and the truth will set you free." John 8:32. You are not free to live as you see fit but the truth gives you the way to live within the limits of God's law.

The Grace of God.

"What is man that you are mindful of him, the son of man that you care for him?" Ps 8:4. Why should God care about you or pay for your sin? You balked at God's right to rule the earth and stuck your finger in his face to say no. What did you do to justify his gift and make Christ go the extra mile for you on Calvary?

You may not understand why God would want to save you but he thought you were worth the trouble that he went through. You may think you are not worthy to know God because you ran from God's grace and sinned. It is the grace of God and his love for you that sought a way to be friends with you. God did not want to see you perish (see 2 Peter 3:9). God sought you by making his love known to you when he died for you. Then by God's grace he supplied your need and made life a gift to those that choose to know him.

God loves you.

The Love God has for you is the same kind of love you have for your own children. God does not find fault with you for when you need his wisdom he answers your prayer with things that you can use. God will stand beside you but he wants you to cast you cares on him so he can help you. God's love for you is not a spur of the moment thing but a plan to help you when you need it, not when he has time. Most of all God's love for you will not force you to obey him but lets you be in charge of your life. His love has your best interest in mind and leaves your dignity in tact.

God Fights Your Battles.

Why did the walls of Jericho fall and how could a David stand up to a man that was going to kill him for the fun of it. Your peers prod you to take that drink or go ahead, take it home, no one will miss it. All of you have been pushed to the brink due to your faith. Why not! Every one else does it. God is always behind the scenes ready to give you the strength to be a man that stands up for what is right. God is also the only one who has beaten Satan time after time. He lives in the realm where Satan is and hates the evil Satan wants you to do. God knows that you can not fight evil alone.

The evil you see man do is not fought on earth or among men but fought at the source. By giving your life to God you gain an ally in the spirit realm who wants to help you live. God knows the conflicts you have and wants to help you resist sin. When you need the help to stand your ground and obey God, he goes to the source of evil that is tempting you and runs Satan off. God enables you to stand when the fiery darts of Satan are flung at you.

God gives you peace.

God gives you a peace that passes any knowledge you may fathom. God has prepared works for you to do that are just, right, and fair for all and those works will give you peace. To know that if you die you will go to live with God forever, that is peace. When you do not have to look over your back to see what your deeds have done that's peace. When you offend no one, that's peace. To know that you will not go to hell, that is peace. By obeying God he grants you peace to sleep. See Ps 127:2.

If you want peace do things that others will agree with. When they can find no fault in you, what do they have to fight over? God tells you to forgive those you are angry with you and show them what they are doing wrong. Settle the dispute so the issue can be put to rest and you will be able to live without creating more problems. God teaches you how to solve life issues and how to live from a heart of love.

God Gives You Time.

One fact is certain you don't know the age of God. God has had the time to know what works and how to do the job right the first time. For you time is a gift but knowing what works and does not work is learned over time. For man, time is an issue that takes place between his birth and his death. Good, bad, or ugly, God will see the character you built in that time. To have influence you must learn to manage the time you have and plan for your future.

Yesterday you played, today you work and tomorrow you will die. Your life is limited and once it is gone you can't change it. How you use that time is in your hands so use it wisely. God said. "It is appointed once for man to live then the judgment." Heb 9:27. Find out what you can do to avoid the coming wrath that God has planned for those who cause and practice evil. God is in control and his plan will work as he said it would. You may want to use your time to "find out what pleases the Lord." Ephesians 5:10. When you know God you will see for yourself why he is so fussy about how you think. Time is limited and you need to use your time to know God while you can find him.

God's Influence on you.

Does God have to shake the earth to get your attention? Do you have to be at the gate of hell to know that you need to get right with God? Why are men loyal to God and ready to die for his cause? The influence God has on you stems on your need for God.

> "God's voice thunders in marvelous ways; he does great things beyond our understanding. He says to the snow, 'Fall on the earth,' and to the rain shower, 'Be a mighty downpour.' So that all men he has made may know his work, he stops every man from his labor. The animals take cover; they remain in their dens."
>
> Job 37:5-8.

Job saw that God had the influence to stop your work in the field so you could find a dry place to stand. Yet the falling rain cleans the air you breathe and give you water to drink. Then God paints a beautiful arch across the sky for you to see. There is no question that God has influence on you but do you listen?

Your influence.

Your influence begins and ends with the way you think. God is dealing with the way you think and the decisions you make. God wants you to benefit from what you put in your mind. Just as you tell your children to share their toys God asks you to share your wealth. God is your father in heaven and he is trying to shape the choices you make, just as you do with your children.

Trust is earned but you have to show the world that you can be trusted. You want a better life but the world deceives you by reducing the value of life to dollars and cents. From the eyes of our Lord, life is precious and what you do either makes life better or worse. God has given you the right to choose the influence that you benefit the most from. When it is all said and done, you have to decide whom to trust.

How has God influenced your life? If you were to think and act like God, you too would be an influence to the world. The events of the past tell the world who the villains were, but tell a lie and your influence will vanish like the morning dew and, what is worse, you may join their ranks. Steal from the world and they will put you away so they can feel safe. Instead of living like the world does, let your friends know that you know God. When they have a problem to solve they can say, Hey I got a friend who knows God, let's go ask him. Listen, your friends can see the light of God in your life and they are hungry for the good news. Use it for God's glory.

CHAPTER 12

Putting Ethics Into Your Character

Have you thought of using the grace of God as a plan to live by? Your character has a high value to God because he is looking for men that think and act the way he does. God lives by love and the love he has for you is shown in the strength of his grace. God wants you to adopt the love he has for others, that you may show the glory of God to man. For you, God's plan is to love those in your life, as you want to be loved. God is saying that the dignity you want, is to give the honor you need from others.

God knows that you have a need to be loved but you have to act accordingly. God not only gave you a way to love but a plan to live in peace. Peace gives you the time to build and make your life better but sin ruins the work you have done. God does not want you to steal, lie, or kill, for these are the deeds that create the spiritual war you have in this world. This kind of war ruins the character. You need respect, honor, and love from others. The plan God has for peace is that you love others, as you would like for them to love you. When you give respect, honor, and love to others you give them the dignity they need for a happy life.

The people you admire the most are willing to help you at anytime of the day or night. They may not like the way you live but they would give you the shirts off their back. God treats you better than you deserve and he wants you to do the same with your fellow man. These are the ideals that God lives by and the way he wants to be loved by you. God wants to teach you his grace so you can conduct your life to be just, right, and fair even to those who hate you.

Most people admire God for the qualities of his grace, and below are some of them.

A.) God is holy and morally pure.
B.) God is an innovator.
C.) God gives dignity to others.
D.) God is the same today yesterday and tomorrow.
E.) God is just, fair to all not impartial.
F.) God is generous.
G.) God considers the needs of others and works for your best interest.
H.) God is humble meek and lowly yet bold.
I.) God comforts you.
J.) God lives by an absolute set of rules.

K.) God is faithful — he is always there for you.
L.) God forgives freely.

The test.

Is it that God needs to know what you stand for or is it that God wants to know if he can trust you? Life forces you to interact with other men and God needs to know what you will you do under stress. These tests give God a picture of your life, so he will know how you think and act. For example, do your best attributes show up when you are angry? If these tests do anything, they turn your life inside out and show what you lack. These tests tell you what you have an attitude adjustment you need to make, but they also let God know if you have a desire to change to please him.

God wants you to behave by his standards and to think as he does. God asks you to think on his word day and night, "so that you may be careful to do everything written in it." Joshua 1:8. The result being, what you think about is what you do. The trial always hits you when you least expect it, but do you focus your attention more on the trial than to please God. By having your mind on the things of God, you are more apt to respond in a godly manner than to focus on how life is treating you. When you spend time with God, he can teach you to rule your life and not let your trials rule what you do.

God is seeking the truth of your core values and he wants to know if you will cross the line. Will you serve God all the time or when you have the time? Will you adopt his ways or continue to live as you see fit? Will you do what's right no matter what it costs you or ignore his law to further your needs? The way you act under stress shows God the core values you have and how you would affect his future plans.

Not long ago I heard a man and wife talking about their son who had moved back home. Their son had washed his clothes, cooked his meal, then cleaned the pots and pans. They knew that their son did not do this in the past and was asking, what does he want? A change of habit will make others stop to see what you are up to. However, God wants to see changes in the way you govern your life.

God has seen the tests you have faced and the affect they had on your life. God has seen what you have done and was with you in the trial. No one likes to pick up the apples to start over again but these tests shape the way the apples are put into your cart. Life has a way to spill the cart and repeat things you did wrong so that you get it right. It is not bad luck that you are tested but it is the time when you learn what to do the next time.

Belief system and core values.

Are you willing to pay ten dollars for a paper clip? For the seller the price is more than he needs but his profit margin is the kind he wants. For the buyer the price is too high and the seller is out to gouge you. Thus, the price is unfair and so high that you will not buy the clip. The price has driven you from the seller and you go home without the paper clip.

Just as you want a fair price, God has core values that are right, just, and fair to all that never change. His core values are his beliefs and the laws that he lives by. As a man, you may have a doctor's degree and the wisdom to earn a living, but to God your ability to think has not matured. The problem is that you think as a man of the world, not as a man of God. As a man of the world you cling to your right to think and act as you see fit. God's law limits you to conduct your life in a positive way. God says, "But solid food is for the mature, who by constant use have trained themselves to distinguish good from evil." Heb 5:14. Your job is to learn to identify good from evil and apply the ideals of God to live in a godly fashion.

You are influenced by what is done to you. Do you like the things that you've worked hard for, taken from you? Why do you want to wrap your hands around the throat of the thief and tightly squeeze it when you have been robbed? Bad core values do not put you in conflict with the act but with the perpetrator. The way you react to those that steal, kill, and destroy your life can make you become as bad as the thief you want to choke. On the other hand, God has the better idea, pray for them, in other terms return good for evil. This brings up a question. How do you feel about those that help you, with what you need, when you need it?

Attitude of Character.

One of the best attitudes of God is in how he

deals with others. God's sees the way you are and he still loves you. That is not an accident, it is an act of his will to love you. God does not look at what you are wearing or how your hair looks. He looks at your heart and the choices you make in life. God knows that you need to make the most of the life with what you have. Time and money are not a factor of God's life but the quality of life is. God has chosen to give his best effort and wants the same from you. When God said, "Thou shalt not," he is telling you to avoid the things that creates strife, kills your joy, and ruins your value to God.

The attitude to love is not the only motive that drives God to live right with others. Love compels you to change the way you think about others and work as one. Love may be the cause of why you agree but two that work for the same goals are stronger. Sin drives people apart, but to forgive your enemy, will make them a friend. Love finds a way to deal with the things that hurt you and, the way you love others shows your need for friends. Love sues for peace because it knows that the strife will not stop unless you deal with the source of violence. "Blessed are the peacemakers, for they will be called sons of God." Matthew 5:9.

Meekness.

Meekness is how you compare yourself to others. Huge egos are hard to deal with, more so when the peon thinks he's the boss? You can have pride with who you are and what you do as long as you give the dignity that others want. To be meek you must give others the respect they need even when they may not merit it. Pride is good when it has limits but meekness lets you see the need of those you are dealing with.

Employers look for docile men that can be molded into the worker they need. He looks for men that are pliable and can put their ways aside to do a professional job for his customers. Any man can be an asset to his employer when he yields to them. By yielding your authority to those in power on your job, your relationship with your boss and with God will only improve.

Dignity is a basic need of God and all men want the same kind of respect. God does not want his name abused but held in awe. Just as God has needs, so do you. You can serve God by letting others become more important than you are. Be willing to go down in rank or lower yourself to help those in need, that will show them God loves them. Just knowing that God loves them may give them a reason to live.

Being Faithful.

There is nothing of more value in life than to have a friend you can count on. You need a friend that you can trust and will be at your side in good or bad times of your life. You also need a friend that you trust enough to share your secrets with. Jesus Christ is a true friend who is like the person you trusted enough to marry. A friend is the one who is not afraid to say, "if you need any help, call me day or night." God lives in you as a constant friend and will help you in your time of need.

God has a set of priorities to keep and stay on top of his word to see that his will is done. He works his plan to remain faithful to those he gave his word to. God wants to be your friend and that is a tall order when you think of everyone he gave his word to. God says that his word will stand forever and his loyalty to his word lets you know that you can trust him. Because of his word you know you have the hope of glory and that you are a child of God. That is how sure God's word is because you know that Christ will come to take you to his home in glory.

Being thankful.

Years ago, I cursed God for the life he gave me and I did not want to obey God. I did not want to go to hell but I did not want to serve God either. The idea that anyone could tell me how to live was not what I wanted. I wanted to be in charge of my life and be the top dog of all I did. I was angry at the world and the choices I made took me down into the pit of despair. I was going to hell not knowing that God wanted to give me life. Now that I know him, my idea of God has changed and I owe him my life. However, with that former attitude I found it hard to say thank you.

I can not remember the words, thank you, being said at home. If my mom and dad taught me those words, my attitude for life made "thank you" hard to say. If anything my father taught me to be self reliant and that I did not need help from anyone. My parents had to force thank you out of my mouth for I was seldom in that mood. Today my attitude has changed because God loves me and he knows how to bless his kids. I still have to make an effort to say thank you, but when God answers my prayers, I get excited with the good things he gives. I am so happy with the gift that I fail to think that the giver has feelings too. His gift was just what I needed and made me feel like I was floating on clouds that I forget to thank God until the joy subsides.

When the thrill is gone, you need to let God know that you approve and love what he did for you. Live your life in such a manner that you let God know that you appreciate him more than the gift. A friend such as God will be around long after the gift wears out, so saying thanks is the way to tell your friend. Stick around, I need you.

Praise.

Actions speak louder than words. God has said that men praise him with their mouth but their heart is far from him. Do you belong to Christ or are you beating the air with your fists? Praise is what you do during the week to say, "Jesus is Lord". You cannot leave your beliefs at the church door to say that you love God. A man that is known to be full of hot air, says one thing and does another. Praise not only has to come from the heart but it has to agree with the way you live.

You have a choice to be thankful or ignore what God has done for you. God asks that you "offer the sacrifice of thanks giving which is the fruit of your lips." Heb 13:15. "The tongue has the power of life and death, and those who love it will eat its fruit." Prov 18:21. You have the choice of the words you speak and the right to say them. Your words can cut to the bone or lift others out of the mire and give them a reason to live. You need to thank God for his help, for without his help you would be lost and have no hope for the future.

God is generous.

Can you out give God when he owns the earth and all that is on it or is it better to give than receive? It would take you a lifetime to go to all the stars that God owns, but the assets of God are more than his huge creation. Your life is a part of what he owns. To keep you from perishing, he gave his Son as a ransom so you could enjoy life with him. This should tell you that God thinks more of you than the rest of the things he owns.

God went the extra mile for you and is able to do more than you can think or imagine. God made other solar systems larger than the one you live in. God can have anything he desires but he wants to know you. You are a speck of dust in size to the earth, but God lavishes his love on you and gave you his spirit without measure. He bestowed the gift of life to you even when you did not deserve it. God does not want you to perish and went the extra mile on Calvary's hill to see that you don't. At Calvary, Jesus gave all he had to give and laid his life down for you.

God love (agape) is a free form of love, but it is not the erotic kind of love you have with a mate. God's love is a love that comes out of the need you have as a man. God gave you a reason to love him and to love others, as you want to be loved. Behind all of this is a generous God who is willing to share what he has with you. Jesus said, "I am come that they might have life, and that they might have it more abundantly." John 10:10 (KJV.) Life is one of those things that God wants to share with you and life in abundance shows the generosity that God has.

Much can be said of the love God has for you. God is known for his graces, so stop and think for a minute. Hasn't God taught you to live by the same grace that God sheds on you? God wants to refine you and mold you into a individual that can govern your life while you respect the rights of others. The traits of others rub off in the time you spend with them. God says it this way. "A little yeast works through the whole batch of dough." Gal 5:9. Use that law to your advantage to allow God's character to work in and through your spirit by spending time with God. God is awesome but when you build his truth and teaching into your life, you will begin to be like God.

CHAPTER 13

Living By Faith

Is God a myth, is there any proof that God exists, did God create the earth, and where did the universe come from? These are questions that men seek answers too. It is easy to explain away these things when you don't believe in God or can't see him. Seeing is believing, but you can see and believe God with the eyes of faith. God is no longer a myth or a fairy tale. When you know him he becomes real to you.

Why go to church or seek a being you can not see? You need to satisfy the questions you have about God and fill the void in your life for God. God gave you eyes to see and ears to hear that work through faith in God. Since you are a spirit being, God gave you eyes and ears that function in the spirit realms as they do in this world. It is your faith in God that opens your eyes to see Christ as your Savior and hear the word of God. You will never know God unless you ask Christ into your heart. Nearly every man on earth believes that God exists but to ask Christ into your life uses your faith in God's word.

Faith is a walk with God.

Faith is not a belief that God exists or the name of the church you go to. It is why you trust in God. The demons know who God is and they shudder when they consider their fate because they know with certainly that God keeps his word. With God for all things is done by faith through Christ. God says, "without faith it is impossible to please God." Heb 11:6. "But my righteous one will live by faith. And if he shrinks back, I will not be pleased with him". Hebrews 10:38.

At work, all you have to do is ask the person you work with if he or she wants to go to heaven when they die. They reply like this. Of course, I hope I have been good enough to go there. Their answer tells you that they do not know God and though you have not seen God or heaven, you do not need any hope to go to there. Rather, you are sure that you will walk on the streets of gold. God has given you the facts and a reason to believe that these facts are as real to you if they had already happened.

Knowing that God has a plan for your future is why you are going to heaven. You know that God has never lied to you and you expect that God will do exactly what he said. Your faith in God knows that no one can snatch you out of God's hand and that is why you have put your life in God's hands.

You trust God so much that you are living by his plan and have made Christ your Lord. You now obey and follow a savior that you have never seen with your eyes but know as a friend. God's plan sounds too good to be true and the idea that God will take you to a place in the age to come where he lives and life never ends, is more than one can fathom. The world has a false sense of hope and while they hope to go to heaven, that hope has no trust in the person of Christ. They believe that Jesus is the Christ, but they don't know that they must be born again.

Faith is a conviction that you accept as true and will grow with use. What is important is that your trust in God will let him guide you through life. Deeds are a result of what you believe and God wants you to rely on him to do his will. The question is, are you willing to trust God's word for what he said he would do?

A Shield of faith.

A shield is a barrier between you and harm. At work, shields are placed at pinch points to protect you from injury while the machine is running. The shield of faith can not be seen but it is a shield that can protect you from evil. When you speak God's word, your faith in God is out in front of you. God's word is the shield that stops the darts that Satan throws at you and puts the sword of God into your hands. God says that, "you live by faith not by sight." 2 Cor 5:7. You can let God's word protect you from harm and you can speak God's word as fluently as the world curses.

Faith comes by hearing.

"So then faith cometh by hearing, and hearing by the word of God." Rom 10:17 KJV. You hear God's word spoken at church and hear the word of God that you and others say. How you react to the words of God will differ by who said them. Words that people speak help a little but when you hear God speak to you, you can move a mountain. Faith gives you the "I can do it courage," to act on the behalf of God. When you hear God speak to you, you have the power of God to step out in faith. God not only gives you the faith to go to work but also equips you to do his will. When you know that you have heard the words of God, you can do the impossible because when God speaks, doubt takes a hike.

The word of God will give you the courage to face your trials with a positive outlook. Just knowing that God is with you will let you face the trial with joy. Since he is at your side, you can run the race knowing that you are going to win. God's word was written so that with the use of his word you can have hope. With Christ at your side, you have a hope and a future that you can look forward to.

Faith works through Christ.

Were there other reasons for God to send Christ, other than to die for your sins? Christ was a man that men could see hear and touch (1 John 1:1). History has a record of a man named Jesus that died on a cross. Jesus was a real man that God used to show that he loved you. God has a plan for you that is focused on Christ and God's word. Christ said this. "Remain in me, and I will remain in you. No branch can bear fruit by itself; it must remain in the vine. Neither can you bear fruit unless you remain in me. "I am the vine; you are the branches. If a man remains in me and I in him, he will bear much fruit; apart from me you can do nothing." John 15:4-5. Christ is the high priest that you use your faith to reach God with. "I am the way and the truth and the life. No one comes to the Father except through me." John 14:6. "I am in my Father, and you are in me, and I am in you." John 14:20. These verses show that you are united to God through your faith in Christ.

God draws all men to Christ by way of the cross, then Jesus leads you to God the Father. "Salvation is found in no one else, for there is no other name under heaven given to men by which we must be saved." Acts 4:12. Christ is the narrow gate you must enter life through by faith. Just to give your life to God shows your trust in the name of Jesus and it was a step of faith. Jesus is the way to God but "it is by the grace of God that you are saved." Eph. 2:8.

Saying that Jesus is your Lord does not make him your Lord. Christ said, "He who does not love me will not obey my teaching. These words you hear are not my own; they belong to the Father who sent me." John 14:24. The plan sounds simple enough but to make Jesus your Lord, you need to do what he asks of you.

Doing the Impossible.

Is faith using God's word to your advantage or is it God using you for his glory? Faith is the trust you have in God when you rely on his promises to meet your needs. Are you willing to use God's word again when you learn how your trial turned out? The trials of your faith will let God polish the rough surfaces of your life. God wants you to rely on him so together great feats can be done. On the other hand, faith works both ways, God relies on you as much or more than you rely on him.

God thinks bigger than you do and the jobs he gives are often more than you can do. God gives you a dream or a vision of the goals he wants you to do and a feasible way to do them. The problem is that you think small and don't see things the way God sees them. God wants to move you into new areas of life that have risks where you have to rely on him. Those risks are mixed with the fear of doing a job that takes you out on a limb. When you do anything for God you have your part and God has his part to do. The part you think as too hard for you to do and out of your control is God's area of expertise. God needs for you to learn to work with him while you grow to the potential of being like Christ.

Look at the size of God's creation and you will see that God thinks on a larger scale than men do. Traveling at the speed of light, it would take you more than a lifetime to cross the space that God created. To you, the jobs God gives you can be just that big. Any job that God gives will affect how you think. God has given you his word to rely on, such as, "Is there anything too hard for God to do?" Gen 18:14, Jer 32:27. "I can do all things through Christ who strengthens me." Philippians 4:13. "Now to him who is able to do immeasurably more than all we ask or imagine, according to his power that is at work within us." Ephesians 3:20. The question is, do you believe him?

Even Christ said, "it is the Father, living in me, who is doing his work." John 14:10. To do God's work you need to use the power of God that is at work in you just as Christ did. However, you have to release the power of God that lives in you. Your faith takes the jobs that are too big for you and lets God handle them. God knows what you can do, but God get all the glory for doing the impossible.

Faith as seen through God's eyes.

Sit on God's side of the table and try to see life as God may see it. God has a past that he can not change just as you do, but he has a future that he can shape by what he does today. In human terms, God does not burn the bridges behind him but plans for his tomorrow. God is working to fulfill his plans and has a job for you to do. God knows that how you think shapes the way you live, but God gave you a set of ideals to build your life with. The principles of God help you to live in such a way that you will have a purpose to fulfill and a way to do them.

You can not change your past but you can have a change of mind. Those in the world do not see the life God wants to give so they live for today. You have the same choice to live for tomorrow as God does. Sin burns the bridges behind you, but faith, hope and love are the tools that build your future. You need to live by faith and believe that you can do all things through Christ. The impossible gives you a challenge to do, a risk to overcome and a reason to live. Life is worth winning the race and with God's help you can do more than men can alone.

The hope God has when you see what sin does to you, will change how you live. God wants you to see how he sees life and use his ideals to live by. Life starts when you learn to think using God's principles to govern your thoughts. This frees you to rule your life and allows you to live in such a way that God can not find fault in you. Paul wrote, "The righteous will live by faith." Rom 1:17. Living by faith then is a belief in God and that his ideals is right for your life. Faith then lets you be an individual, helps you to rule your life, and encourages you lean on God for help. Most of all, faith lets you please God with your actions.

Your Faith will be opposed.

Why do things go bad when you put a perfect plan to work? In football, eleven men try to carry a ball from one end of the field to the other while eleven other men do their best to stop them. In war men fight hard to take the high ground but those on the hill do their best to keep it. When you want to do things for God, Satan is going to stop you before you take your first step. Satan wants you to think that God did little if anything for you and he has a plan to make you think that God's word is all a hoax. That is why you must take a stand by yielding to God.

The moment you became a Christian you stepped into a war between good and evil. The fight of faith is a war that you can not see with your eyes but is fought in the spirit realm. Satan, who is God's enemy, is out to choke or steal the word of truth from you. He will have you doing things the way the world does, until you know the truth. Then he will keep you busy working for the things that God hates. The moment you start to do things for God, Satan gets in your face with the reasons to change your mind. Suddenly a feeling comes over you that makes you think that the world is going to reject you. Satan is out to stop you and he will do anything he can to keep you from doing the good that God wants you to do.

Building your faith.

There is only one way to know for sure your faith in God is valid and that is to taste and see that the Lord is good. Try his word out by using his word to achieve your goals. Then sit back and wait to see if God will keep his word to you. One thing for sure is that you will not worship a god that does not keep his word.

Many stories have been told to illustrate faith.

This is one, where a few years ago a drought was about to ruin the crops in a town west of here. The farmers of the town set a time of prayer to ask God for rain, but when they met in the church, one man stood out from all the others. He had an umbrella in his hand. His faith in God told him that he would be drenched on the way home.

Do you expect to get an answer from God when you pray? God seeks the truth in you but the truth is shown by the way that you react to God's word. "If you believe, you will receive whatever you ask for in prayer." Matt 21:22. Keeping his word is one of God's priorities so God watches to see that his word is done (Jer 1:12). You have the promise of God that he will do what he said he would do.

Satan has a bad attitude and opposes the goals of God. Satan couldn't care less if you want to live and if you were to perish, so what! As god of this world he has a grip on the way you live and his influence has a power that compels you to sin. You are God's child and you need to set your mind on the things above to become the image of Christ. God is a strong influence, but to be like Christ, you need to change the way you think and act. Be open to God's word by letting the truth of his word do its work.

Keeping your word.

"You have seen correctly, for I am watching to see that my word is fulfilled." Jer 1:12. At times, God's word seems to be too good to be true. On the other hand, Satan will do his best to prove that God's word is a lie all to help you fall. Nothing would give Satan more pleasure than to see you fall in sin. His aim is to kill your trust in God and to make you his slave.

How do you feel when others can not trust your word? They know that you have good intentions but they can't count on you. People that rely on your word know how you have kept your word in the past. Your past has told them that you did or did not live up to your word. At times you need help to get the job done, but you cannot rely on the good intentions of others? This is the reason that God watches his word so that when you reach out for God's help, you get his help. You can make promises but do you make the effort to keep your word? God knows that his words are empty when he does not keep them. Instead he promises that his word will not return to him void. He makes an all out effort to be sure that he keeps his word by performing them.

The man with the umbrella made plans for rain and went to town to pray for rain. He came prepared and by using his faith in God, he could count on God to meet his needs. He opened his umbrella and held it above his head on the way home showing the world his trust in a great God that answers prayer. Do you have this kind of faith in God? Does your faith rely on God to keep his word?

CHAPTER 14

Making Binding Agreements That Work

In our town, a City Park sign reads that all dogs must be on a leash and curbed. When you are in this park and walking a dog, by law, a leash must be on any dog with you. Like men, dogs have a mind of their own and they want to do things their way. The leash has two ends, one for you and one for the dog. The question is, will you take the dog for a walk or will the dog take you for a spin?

Your dog doesn't know that he is unruly because dogs live by instinct. They let their nose guide them to food and to places you don't want to know about. When they smell things that interest them, you are off to the races. For some dogs you may wonder how that leash keeps your dog and you out of trouble.

The leash just seems to be more trouble than it is worth but with other dogs, you have good reason to obey the law.

Taking the dog for a walk has always been a good excuse for exercise. Putting the leash on your dog will not allow you to control of the dog, but if you don't, that is when the dog will do everything but obey you. The leash only connects you to the dog but it's how you use the leash that controls the dog. The leash is just a tool to ensure the dog agrees to your needs. The dog is still free to drag, push or pull you, as long as he is on the leash.

The key to control of the dog seems to be in the length of the leash. Keeping the leash short keeps the dog at your side and when the dog is at your side he will walk with you. Let him have the leash and he will pull you where he wants to go. In some way your dog is like your kids. Both the dog and your kids will go to the extent of their leash to test you just to see what they can get away with.

All dogs must be on a leash and curbed or at least that is what the sign at the park said. Curbed is a term that demands restraint or has limits, but a dog can be on a leash and not be curbed. When the dog is not curbed, he is in control. The dog can not be allowed to chew on the things he passes, nor can he be allowed to chase the stray cat. People need order in life and a way to be safe from the dog that lives by his instincts.

For any restraint on the dog to be in force you have to be in charge. Should the dog stray off, yank on the leash to remind the dog that you are on the other end. The use of the leash keeps the dog's attention on your needs and is the terms that the dog has to agree with.

The effects of binding.

When two or more join to do a job, you need to agree on how the job is done and who does what. Binding is a way to agree that limits what you do and compels you to do that job. In most cases you can't see, feel or touch the form of binding that you will use in your lifetime. However, the truth is that you are on a leash.

Walking the dog shows you how men live with each other. You may have a plan to do something but other people do the very thing that clashes with your plan. Why is it, that what's right for you differs from the one who yanks on your leash. On the job, you have agreed to do the work their way. The boss has you on a leash and can tell you where you go and what to do. Should you speed on the way home the policeman will yank on your leash and hand you a ticket. When you get home your spouse yanks your leash telling you to take the trash out. It may seem like everyone has his or her hand on your leash ready to yank. However, there is another end to your leash, on payday its your turn to yank on the bosses leash for your check.

On the other hand, you have your leash in your hand and you are more than ready to hand your leash to others. You need a TV set and you are ready to hand your leash to the bank. Then your spouse yanks on your leash and says we can't afford it. When you buy the TV set you hand the leash of both you and your spouse over to the bank. Giving your leash to other people helps you to reach an agreement where your needs and theirs are met. When you don't keep your part of the agreement they yank on your leash. The yank reminds you of things that you have neglected, miss a payment and who gets a notice. Do something that your spouse does not like and what do they do? The reason for the yank is to remind you of what you agreed to do.

Binding gives two parties a means to be on the same page and a way to work for the same goal. Most agreements have ways that force you to keep a commitment. The penalty of the law gave you an incentive to agree, so you put a leash on the dog. The city thought that a leash would force the owner to control the dog, yet you have to work for the city's goal to avoid the penalty.

"Do two walk together unless they agree to do so?" Amos3:3. The moment you give your life to him, God gives you his commitment that he will be with you until the end of the age. Think of your love, as a leash that binds you to God with two ends. The cords that bind you to God are your word, your love and your faith. God will lead you on a path to a holy life but it will be your love for God that compels you to follow him. Your faith will let you follow God but you need to agree with God or you may feel the yank of the leash.

God uses the principle of binding.

God bound you to a body, a soul, a mind, and a spirit. God gave you a spirit to subdue the other parts of your being that you may rule your life in strength. You were born on earth where other beings allow its flesh to rule his or her life. However, God sees you from the spirit realm and deals with you as a spirit. God is a spirit and you were born of the spirit even though you are confined to the flesh. Yet, God does not want the flesh to rule your spirit because, those who are led by the flesh are concerned with the needs of the flesh. "Those who are led by the Spirit of God are sons of God." Rom 8:14. God is working with the spirit of man, which is the common link that binds God to men.

God loves all men for who they are, but he has limited his presence to those who give their heart to him. God's love for man drove Christ to a hill where he was lifted up to pay for the sins of man. By his death Christ showed that he does not want anyone to perish but be saved from his sin. When you accept Christ's death on the cross as the penalty for your sins, God hands you his end of the leash. By taking that leash, you hand your life over to Christ and with love he will lead you into God's presence.

Binding is a way to share your life to work with others. Do you think a bear will have any trouble knowing what's for lunch when you grab his leash? "Do two walk together unless they have agreed to do so?" Amos 3:3. The leash gives you the right to lead the bear, but only if the bear is willing. The leash is the authority to your life and when you hand it to anyone, you give your consent for others to temporarily rule your life. Did you give your life to God of your free will with the hope that God will save you from the fire? You gave your word to serve God and by your word you hand your end of the leash to God.

God gave you the right to use his name and the promises of his word. "You may ask me for anything in my name, and I will do it." John 14:14. God's word is his bond and you can yank on his leash for him to perform his word for you. All a part of the agreement he is willing to make with you when you agree to obey him.

God has put his Spirit in your heart as a deposit of what is to come. God has placed his seal on you, not only to say you belong to him but also to guide you. When you let the spirit of God lead you, you will have the power of God to resist evil. The Holy Spirit is a guide to the truth, helping you to know the one and only true God. God uses his spirit to keep you in line with his word and when you are about to stray into sin, he will warn you. God wants you to know that he will work with you so you can win the race of life.

God binds with you to help you.

Just as you have plans to do things with your life God does all things with a plan. "For I know the plans I have for you," declares the LORD, "plans to prosper you and not to harm you, plans to give you hope and a future." Jer 29:11. You can choose a life with God, or gloom and doom in hell, but God does not want or plan for you to perish. Instead, God wants you to repent from a life that leads to death and use his plan of salvation to change the way you think and act. God wants you to prosper in everything you do so you can have a hope and a future with God. God's plan is. "Do not let this Book of the Law depart from your mouth; meditate on it day and night, so that you may be careful to do everything written in it. Then you will be prosperous and successful." Josh 1:8. The only way you can have hope and a future is to work his plan.

God's plan to help you prosper is a plan to change the way you think and act. The process that is shown in Joshua 1:8 is a plan that will make you successful. Your spirit will see how to live with the help of the Holy Spirit who is your mentor that will teach you how to become like Christ. Christ said this, "Take my yoke upon you and learn from me, for I am gentle and humble in heart, and you will find rest for your souls. For my yoke is easy and my burden is light." Matt 11:29-30. The yoke does what the leash did to connect you to God but now you and Christ are a team. Take my yoke, join with me to learn from me the secrets of the kingdom that will change the way you think and act.

No one will force you live to by his plan even though God hands you his leash with promises. Taking his leash is your opportunity to agree with God, and a way to commit your life to him. God will work with you saying, "You, dear children, are from

God and have overcome them, because the one who is in you is greater than the one who is in the world." 1 John 4:4. God is in you to make you stronger, to share your life, to help make sound choices, and guide your steps by casting his light on your path. Therefore, you can live the kind of life and be the person that God can proudly say, "This is my Son, whom I love; with him I am well pleased." Matt 3:17.

You can bind to God.

God said "man did not live by bread alone but by every word that comes from the mouth of the Lord." Deut 8:3. God is saying that you need other kinds of food, than food for your body since you live by the word he speaks. Bread is the fuel that makes your body function, but the bread of the spirit is the knowledge you need to live by. "The fear of the LORD is the beginning of knowledge" Prov 1:7, "but the advantage of knowledge is this: that wisdom preserves the life of its possessor." Eccl 7:12. "If any of you lacks wisdom, he should ask God, who gives generously to all without finding fault, and it will be given to him." James 1:5. By binding to God you gain the benefit of knowledge that leads to life.

God is ready and willing to keep you abreast with his wisdom. Once you give your life to God, you place your life into his hands. It is his desire to keep you safe, his wish to make you holy, and one day receive you in his home. Binding with God is a win, win situation when you want to live.

Binding to God is not a one sided deal that God

saves your life just for saying a few words. You have a major part in your agreement with God just to keep your word. God wants you to, "Seek first his kingdom and his righteousness, and all these things will be given to you as well." Matt 6:33. Then, "Everyone who hears these words of mine and does not put them into practice is like a foolish man who built his house on sand." Matt 7:26. You want to be saved from God's wrath but you must commit your life to find out what pleases the Lord and then do it.

Committing your life to God.

Being bound to a chair will force you to be part of the chair but the chair attached to you will limit what you can do. When you gave your life to Christ you were united with God not with ropes but with a vow. The vow you gave God to serve him the rest of your life and it is a lifetime commitment that you need to respect. God will take you seriously and expect you to keep your word. God's word places limits on you so you will follow him and a Christian has a life of discipline. "Sin is crouching at your door; it desires to have you, but you must master it." Gen 4:7. Sin is at your door all day long yet you need a resolve to keep your life right with God at any cost. "So then, dear friends, since you are looking forward to this, make every effort to be found spotless, blameless and at peace with him." 2 Pet 3:14. Making every effort is not casual everyday life, it is all out effort to shun evil. It is a plan to live right before God till the day he comes for you. Job said, "What will I do when God confronts me? What will I answer when called to account?" Job 31:14. God takes the vows you made to him seriously and you need to do the same.

Being of one accord.

Following the Last Supper Jesus prayed the following prayer found in John 17. The crux of his prayer focused on one goal. "Father, just as you are in me and I am in you. May they also be in us so that the world may believe that you have sent me. I have given them the glory that you gave me, that they may be one as we are one: I in them and you in me. May they be brought to complete unity to let the world know that you sent me and have loved them even as you have loved me." John 17:21-23.

God wants to work with you to let the world know that he has sent you to tell the world that he loves them. God gave you a job to do with the great commission and he lives in you to give you the power to testify to the truth. He also helps you to work with the rest of the church through the bond of peace.

As Christians, you need to serve God with the rest of his family. Draw up a plan that meets God's goals and commit to work with God as a Church for a goal. That goal is easier to reach when the entire church works for the same goal. The need to unite in the church to work with God as one man is given in the story of Babel. "Then nothing they plan to do will be impossible for them." Gen 11: 6. When you agree with some part of the plan you will be in one accord with the church and with God.

Look at the oneness of God. Jesus said, "When you have lifted up the Son of Man, then you will know that I am [the one I claim to be] and that I do nothing on my own but speak just what the Father has taught me. The one who sent me is with me; he has not left me alone, for I always do what pleases him." John 8:28-29.

Jesus wanted to agree with God and did what he saw God doing. He chose to speak the words his father taught him to say. Jesus worked with God with one mind and one goal. Jesus' life was a success when he became the Lamb of God to reconcile man to God on the cross.

Spending time with God is the most practical way to bind to God. By knowing God and his word you begin to think and act like him. God's plan was that you become the image of Christ and that you would do the works that he did. When you know God, you will know why God does not do things to hurt others. Instead God wants to serve your needs and build a relationship that will last forever. God wants you to unite with him to tell the world that he loves them and does not want them to perish. "Work out your salvation with fear and trembling, for it is God who works in you to will and to act according to his good purpose." Phil 2:12. God will not force you to do his will but when you bind with God you will want to do his will.

CHAPTER 15

Enduring Verses Shrinking Back

Shrinking back is a way to run from evil in a similar fashion that plastic shrinks when in contact with heat. You can run from the heat of the battle and from the fear of being hurt. You may run from the fear of the unknown or what the devil can do, but fear can paralyze you. You have risks in your life and given time, you can look like the plastic that has shrunk in the fire. You can endure the heat of life, but with not without God or hope in your life.

Don't get me wrong, plastic will stand up to heat but will retreat to a point that it can endure the heat. In like manner, you shrink from those who vent their rage at you. Where do you want to be when an angry person is venting their rage? Do you retreat, want to hide, or get out of the way when anger is spewed at you?

You live in an evil world that wants to control you and there is no place to be safe from evil. You have an enemy that you can not see with your eye and no place to hide. Satan keeps you busy with trials and things that come into your life. Trials take your mind off the job God wants you to do and places your mind on your needs. In addition, trials can snuff out the fire of faith you need to survive and makes you withdraw like plastic from the fire.

Where do you stand in your fight of faith, have you had to endure pain for your faith? Church potlucks are of no concern to Satan. The fire is out in the world where the game of life is played, where evil is so common that you no longer consider it as sin. The world has places to go, have things to do and things to buy. They are kept on the run, and without knowing it, are on fire for everything Satan puts in their mind.

God has given you a plan for your life that gives you a hope that the world does not have. "Small is the gate and narrow the road that leads to life." Matt 7:14. Veering to the right or the left of the narrow road will take you off the path to eternal life. Satan has a plan too and will lead onto the road to death.

Jesus said. "In this world you will have trouble. But take heart! I have overcome the world." John 16:33. "If they persecuted me, they will persecute you also." John 15:20. Cheer up, Christ ran the race that you are now running and won. He has promised to run at your side asking you to trust him so you can win the race too. Without God, you can not stand up to the trials but with God you will have what it takes to be with God for the rest of your life.

Prevailing.

In your walk with God there will always be evil in the way to stop you. They make you wonder if it is worth the trouble you have to go through. You can not let those things stop you, or keep you from living right with God. To endure when hard times come you must learn to prevail, the problems you have, just will not go away. You have to take control when troubles explode at your door. You may be able to go around the trouble, but it will come back to haunt you later. Facing the trouble head on is the only way to stay on the path to life. No trouble is so big but that your trust in God will give you the fortitude to face them.

You may think that the odds are stacked in favor of the world. There are times when the pressure to walk the path with God is more than you can bear. "No temptation has seized you except what is common to man. And God is faithful; he will not let you be tempted beyond what you can bear. But when you are tempted, he will also provide a way out so that you can stand up under it." 1 Cor 10:13. You do make a difference in a corrupt world but you can not be like the world. You have to stand out from the crowd like a sore thumb and be the salt of this world. Let your light shine in this dark world where you live so the world knows that God loves them.

Satan will make your life hard because you serve the only true God. The people of this world are blind to the light of the gospel and aid the work of Satan. They do what they feel is right for them, or do the same things that they see others get away with. Some think that Satan is behind all the evil in life, while others blame you for their sin. The world is in the claws of Satan and you can be in his path if you live the way the world does.

God sent Jesus with a plan for his life and he became the model to live by. God's plan for Jesus was to settle the sin issue, but to complete this job for God Jesus had to die. Jesus knew God's plan for his life and he had the power to walk away from the cross. He chose to endure the cross for you and at Gethsemane, Christ fought the hardest battle of his life. Jesus asked God to take the cup away that he was about to drink. The thought of death was on his mind and his death on the cross may have frightened him. The plan God had for his life was working but Christ was looking at the death he faced. Then he said, "Father, if you are willing, take this cup from me; yet not my will, but yours be done." Luke 22:42. Christ trusted his father's desire enough to do God's will at the cost of his life.

No one wants to fail since success is as much a part of God's life as it is for you. God has decided to make his ways and the things he creates to endure as long as he does. Look at what God has created? The water you drink, the air you breathe, and the sun has existed since the beginning of the earth. God does not live in a throw away realm and the life he creates will last for an eternity. You were not created to die but to live forever. You need to succeed in a world that is out to kill, steal, and destroy what you think as life.

The world you live in is evil and nothing will stop evil from being at your door. Satan is at war with God and you, but God has a plan for you to stand in the face of temptation. God's word lets you see good and evil for what it is and his word gives you a sieve to sort sin out of your life. Giving God's word a priority in your life gives you a way to control your life and a good way to shun evil. God says that his word will stand forever because it is the truth. God has given you a way to stand knowing that when you use his word, God watches his word to see that it does exactly what he said it would do. God has given you a way but you have to endure to the end and be found worthy of his calling.

Working for God.

Wicked men suppress the truth and their life shows how easy it is to get by without God to live in sin. They appear to be to be doing well without God and they have the best and the latest. If they want something, they go for it. They do not care what they have to do to get the things that make their life easy. The way they go about getting those things tells you what they think of you and what life is all about. The truth is that you want the same things but you are limited to live a life acceptable to God.

When people are saved, you will hear the words, when I found out or when I heard. God has told you to go and teach the world the very things he taught you to do. When you go, you will find out all the strange things that the world believes in because they are too busy to know the truth. They say "They are not interested or that's not the way the real world works." Satan lets you feel his anger when you hear "leave me alone." You stop short of telling the good news under the guilt trip that Satan lays on you. Remember that it is not your job to force your beliefs on anyone but to take the message of God to the world.

Out in the world you find the bulk of Christians leave their beliefs at the church door. You can't tell them apart from the lost for they talk of Jesus only when they have to and they run with the crowd. To endure as a Christian you have to do what the Christian does, tell the good news. Take the talent that God gave you and build his kingdom for your Lord. Jesus said. "Whoever has my command and obeys them, he is the one who loves me." John 14:21. Lead a man to the Lord and you will feel as if you are walking on cloud nine. The joy of God is not left at the church door but you have to take your joy to the world so the world can see God in you.

Bearing fruit.

> "Listen! A farmer went out to sow his seed. As he was scattering the seed, some fell along the path, and the birds came and ate it up. Some fell on rocky places, where it did not have much soil. It sprang up quickly, because the soil was shallow. But

> when the sun came up, the plants were scorched, and they withered because they had no root. Other seed fell among thorns, which grew up and choked the plants, so that they did not bear grain. Still other seed fell on good soil. It came up, grew and produced a crop, multiplying thirty, sixty, or even a hundred times." Then Jesus said, "He who has ears to hear, let him hear."
>
> Mark 4:3-9.

God's word has to fall on good soil for it to bear fruit. Stones and weeds destroy the root system of the plant and will not let God's word thrive. The seed is bent on growing but the condition of your heart is vital to the seed. The stones or the hardness of your heart and the weeds of sin must be removed from your heart. Plant the word of God into you heart for the nutrients you need to grow. When the winds and the rains come, you will stand under its stress. Like the house built on the rock, the plant will stand up to the trials it has to face.

Keep going.

One thing at a time happens until you are worn out. You relax and you let one thing go by, then another. Before you know it you are in sin. At this point, you can stay in sin or go to God and ask him to forgive you. "If we confess our sins, is faithful and just and will forgive us our sins and purify us from all unrighteousness." 1 John 1:9. When you let the world go by, you will go with it but to endure you have do something to resist the flow. You either sink or swim, but if you swim, you don't always have to start over.

God has made a way for you to endure the race of life. By now you know that God did not give you a bed of roses or the perfect life. Jesus said that if you follow him you would be persecuted. It's not that the world hates you but it's that the world hates the truth of God's word. The truth makes you different and sets you free to choose the way you walk. With Jesus, you have the power of truth to live in this world and he that endures to the end will be saved. Jesus is a light to your path and the words he speaks are life and spirit. It's God's word that can strengthen you to endure to the end of the age.

The idea of enduring to the end tells you that you have to cross the finish line. You have a goal to reach but you have to overcome many trials in life to get there. How you deal with trials is a part of the race you ran and you may feel as if the world is out to get you. Joseph must have felt like this when his brothers threw him into the well. Then he was sold to a slave trader and resold to Potiphar, the captain of the Pharaoh's guard. Joseph used the skills God gave him and served the captain of the guard. In his trial he rose in rank and was put in charge of captain's house. The captain's wife lusted after him but Joseph knew the limits God gave him and ran. The desire the Potiphar's wife once had for him turned to hate and she lied to her husband to get even. Her husband vented his anger on his trusted servant and once more Joseph saw that living for God was not easy.

Life throws curves at you, Joseph was put in the dungeon of pharaoh for doing what was right in God's eye. What a let down, "I did everything right so why am I here?" God, Why me? Many times during his life in Egypt Joseph stood on shaky ground wondering what would happen next. Wondering what else would go wrong, is God out there, and is it worth the trouble to live for God? The questions that go through your mind may be the same that was in Joseph's mind. All he knew was that God had a reason for his suffering.

Then Joseph rose in the ranks again and was put in charge of the prison. God used him in the prison to comfort those in jail during this time. He once told the cupbearer and the baker's what their dream meant and they took place just as he said it would. Then Pharaoh had a dream and found out that Joseph had revealed the meaning of dreams before. Pharaoh asked Joseph to tell what his dream meant and with God's help he did. The result was that Joseph made second only to the Pharaoh. Joseph was true to God without knowing what God had in mind.

During this time Joseph had every reason to give up for it seemed like every time he had success, the world slapped him in the face and he had to start over. Those that thrive in life lose as often as they win but they keep going. When they fall, they get backup and put their eyes back on the goal and go. Try saying this when you go to work. Today is the day the Lord has made and with his help I will shine like the sun! Each day set your goal to be God's light in this world.

Enduring the battle.

Satan is the most enduring of all the woes you face in life, yet you have the right to say no to him. With Jesus, Satan was just a pest that left only for the right time to so he could set his trap. Satan is an enemy that will be at your door ready to catch you off guard. The instant you let your guard down he will leap on you with the zeal of a hungry lion. Even when you yield to God, he will sneak back when you relax. Satan is out to get you any way he can and he will use any way that will sever you from God.

How do you resist a spirit that you cannot see but is out to harm you? Satan is out to steal your life, to destroy your worth to God, and to lead you to your death. You need the truth in your spirit to resist or shun evil in any form. The work you do to put God's word into your spirit will give you a platform of truth to resist evil from. Truth is the only way to fight deceit but God's word has to be in your spirit. By seeking God through his word you build you worth to God and learn what God stands for. You learn why he is strong and when you apply his methods to your life, you will have a high value to God. God knows what you are up against and have equipped you with the means to resist evil.

Managing your life to subdue the world.

Being a Christian is not as easy as one thinks for you live in the world that opposes the way God wants you to live. The world has its own way to live that appears to work. Yet the world turns on you and calls you a fanatic, a fool when you try to show them the word of God. They think that a good person will be saved from the fire and from their eyes, hope they're good enough. Since you have to work out your salvation with fear and trembling, you know that there is more to being a Christian than being a good person.

You can give yourself an A+ for assuming you're a good person but God gives the final grade from his sight. Your salvation and whether you go to heaven is a plan that God has laid out in his word. You have a way to find out what the Lord expects of you. You can agree to change your life to satisfy God's need. Ezekiel said it this way, "Listen carefully and take to heart all the words I speak to you." Ezek 3:10. God wants you to spend time in his presence to learn what he wants you to do. Being a good father, he will chastise you when you sin. God shows you what you did wrong and when he's has your attention he will show you the right way to live.

You have a limited time in which to manage your life and a race to run. Trials use the time and assets that you have to manage so live as wisely as your knowledge permits. So go to work, get your wisdom from God as much as possible and find some one you can trust for good advice. "Bless those that use you and return good for the evil you receive. Be joyful always; pray continually; give thanks in all circumstances, for this is God's will for you in Christ Jesus. Do not put out the Spirit's fire; do not treat prophecies with contempt. Test everything. Hold on to the good. Avoid every kind of evil." 1Thes 5: 16-22. These are the things God wants you to do to manage your life wisely.

CHAPTER 16

Standing Firm In The Heat Of The Battle

God enables you to stand in your trial so you may learn to work with him. God will show you how to stand in his strength with Bible study the work you do with him. Your desire to know God will shorten the time needed to equip you with the truth and build a platform to stand from. Living by God's word takes resolve and the sacrifice of your will. The study of God's word will build your life on the solid rock of Christ. Your stance will be established when Christ is at your side teaching you how to run the race.

Taking a stand is not easy. For you can count on Satan to make your life confusing. God will help you to live right but Satan will make you wonder, what is right? Satan will shower you with his lies until you give in because Satan's goal is to stop you, wear you out, hinder you and cause you to back slide. Shrinking back, hiding, or running from life are methods that gives you a way to avoid taking a stand. To stand firm in the midst of the trial, you need to focus on your goal and to rely on God for help. Keeping your mind on the things above, Bible study will help you to become firm and make a strong stand for God. Knowing the truth and who to trust is the way to a firm stand.

Satan's goal.

A kingdom needs an area to rule and a king to rule it and God gave you a realm to rule made of flesh and blood. Christ came into your life as king when you gave your life to Christ. Since he is your king, God wants you to live by the laws of the kingdom. God's goal is to have you change your mind to forsake your evil ways. God's plan allows you to serve him of your free will and with his plan he will help you repent of the evil that rots the fabric of your life.

Satan is sly, not stupid, he knows the right lies to make you fall from God's grace. "When he lies, he speaks his native language, for he is a liar and the father of lies." John 8:44. Satan roars like a lion to make you cringe and run for cover. Satan is ruthless, doing things that will keep you off guard and ensure that you will fall. Satan knows what occurs when you submit to God but he would rather run and fight another day.

Satan is the ultimate tyrant who wants to be god, and have you as his slave. In his kingdom, there is no choice and you are forced to do evil deeds. The war you fight is not over who is god but whom you trust and let shape your life. God gives you the freedom to serve him of your free will and Satan uses the fallen state of man to own you. God said, "All have sinned and fall short of the glory of God." Rom 3:23. Satan owns you as long as you sin but only if you let him rule your life.

Whom will you serve?

Life in the kingdom of God begins when you gave your life to God. At that time it was a struggle to give your life to God since Satan had his hands on you and you did not know it. God gave you the strength to make that choice and with that choice you overcame the world. God set you free, you became a new creature and now that he is your God, the choices you have are limited to God's rules. You now have to discipline your choices to serve God since Satan is at war with God, and will stop at nothing to get you back.

You did not know that you were in a war with God when you were a sinner. You went with the flow that you saw, heard, and did what the world does. The truth severed you from the world and from Satan who ruled the way you thought and lived. Just as you had trouble making the decision to give your life to God you will have a hard time to live a godly life. Satan can not snatch you out of God's hand but he will tempt you to leave the protection of God's hand to sin. When you gave your life to God you changed sides but now you are in a fight of faith. God does not want you to fight Satan but to resist evil by yielding to God.

"Don't you know that when you offer yourselves to someone to obey him as slaves, you are slaves to the one whom you obey." Rom 6:16. God will not share his right to rule your life with Satan since there is no other god. Paul said that life was a fight of faith and the main question is whom you trust. God needs your trust to serve him with all of your being, of your free will, and has a feasible plan for you to work. When you obey God you make the choice to serve God, but you sin to obey Satan. To serve God you have to stay focused and set your mind to serve God.

A solid stand.

God wants you to have a firm grip on your life like that of a table. A table has legs to stand on and when placed in a room will not move. When you walk in the room you will not affect the table and it will not change its position. The table can only be moved when an outside force is used to move it from its place. God wants your grip to be so firm that nothing outside of him can change what you believe.

God does not want you to change your mind constantly or sit on both sides of the fence. God wants to know if you are for him or against him, but the qualities of wavering make God wonder where you stand. God wants you to make the distinction that shows where you stand on good and evil. God works from an absolute principle of truth and made laws that he has chosen not to violate. God's word says that, "God does not change." Mal.3: 6, and "Jesus Christ is the same yesterday and today and forever." Heb 13:8. "He who is the Glory of Israel does not lie or change his mind; for he is not a man, that he should change his mind." 1 Sam 15:29. God has made his need clear to man that he wants you to change your mind to think the way he does.

God does not give you a foundation that is shaky but a solid rock to work from. The use of God's word teaches you how good and evil differs. You are less likely to doubt or waver when you have the firm knowledge of the truth and you have to rely on God when you stand on his word. You need his strength so study his word till no one can change your mind and then apply it. The wind blows and the rain will come, but the rock of Christ cannot be moved. "So then, just as you received Christ Jesus as Lord, continue to live in him, rooted and built up in him, strengthened in the faith as you were taught." Col 2:6-7.

Choosing to be firm.

The greatest gift God gave to man was the right to make his own choices. The Bible tells many stories of those that stood firm and relied on God. Some died of full age and full of vigor but there were also men that chose life without God and went to the grave in ruin. These stories show you how to set goals for your life.

God hates indecision more so when you sin, run to God and then sin again. The changing of mind over who you serve is wavering. Waves come in and go out all day and your mind can change in like manner. God wants to know where you stand whether you are going or coming. God says, "He who is not with me is against me, and he who does not gather with me scatters." Matt 12:30. God has a specific way to deal with others to know what they stand for, there are no gray areas, either you are for or against him.

"I know your deeds that you are not cold or hot. I wish you you're one or the other! Since you are lukewarm I am about to spit you out of my mouth." Rev 3:15-16. To God you are the fruit of the earth and the temperature affects its taste. Being lukewarm is a picture that is a blend of hot and cold and like that of wavering. Perhaps what God is saying that some of the time, you are hot and other times you are cold. Heat affects the taste of food and some are better hot than cold. The trials you face put you through the fire to refine your ways. Are you resolved to serve God and does your life show the temper marks of the heat. Have your robes been washed in the blood or are they stained with sin. Your deeds not only show God how you think and act but where you stand to good and evil.

Anyone who enjoys the better parts of the two worlds is double minded. The man who wants the best of the spirit world and things of the world does not love God. Instead, he is straddling the fence of life and death. Goals are lost when you change sides of the fence for each step every two minutes. There are no rules to walk in the world but to walk in the spirit you need to live by the laws of the kingdom. Straddling the fence of life means that you will obey God when you are on his side of the fence. Only, God does not want you to change your mind with the wind but to have a plan for your life and stick with it. Going back and forth from good to evil makes your life unstable and God wants to know if you want good more than evil.

The price of stocks and bonds change with the news of the day and fads change with the drop of a hat. The trees bend with the wind and Satan changes his lie to fit your needs. Going with the flow can make your life choices shaky at best and the events of your life can radically change the way you think and act. God wants reliable people he can trust so you need to build your life upon the rock that gives you the stability that God wants. Stocks and bonds change their value with the news of the day but you can rely on God's word that will never change.

The armor of God makes you firm.

You have been given the ability to stand firm in the day of trial in his power. To resist the evil of your trial, you need the truth of God's word. God gave you his son and his spirit so that who ever believes in him would not perish but have life eternal. "Now it is God who makes both us and you stand firm in Christ." 2 Cor 1:21. God has given you his word and his armor but you have to use it by putting his word in you. Paul gave this advice, "Put on the full armor of God so that you can take your stand against the devil's schemes." Eph 6:11.

The belt of truth is the foundation of the armor that covers the waist and the hips of the soldier. The belt of truth was the first thing the soldier put on for his life depended on what he carried. The sword was held at the side of the belt by a sheath and kept the sword within reach. Like the soldier, you will never know when you will need the sword on the job. Put the belt that makes the foundation of truth on, so you can serve God in spirit and in truth.

God's armor for the chest and back was put on like the breastplate that was bound to the priest. It was made of two pieces that covered the man from the neck to the waist. The breastplate of the Priest was made in a similar fashion but like a pocket it held two stones (Urim and Thummin) used to know the will of God. God's armor covers your body and the temple of God where God lives by his spirit. God lives in your body as your mentor to help you live and to work as a team in the fight of faith.

The feet are covered with the gospel, like the shoes that did not wear out in the desert. The shoe protects you from the heat of the world and you use your feet to carry the good news to the world. The man who shares good news will go places and is ready to give the good news to those God loves. The good news is that Jesus died for your sin and by his death you have been reconciled to God.

All trials hit you square in the face but the shield of faith keeps you from being wounded. The shield of faith is a barrier that you place out in front of you to protect you from the lies of the enemy. Your faith gives you an edge over those who do not have any protection but when Satan flings lies at you, the truth will quench the lies. You let the word of God flow from your mouth to put the shield of faith out in front of you but when Satan speaks, he flings his darts of lies at you. Remember, "Every word of God is flawless; he is a shield to those who take refuge in him." Prov 30:5. The trust you have in God's word is in knowing God that he stands behind his word. He is the shield to those who take refuge in him. Trials may strike you but God is your refuge when you use the shield of faith.

The sword is used by the man of God to take and hold ground. The sword is seen in the image that God gave of Christ, coming out of his mouth. It was the word that God gave Christ to speak and his words were spirit and life to all men. This sword can pierce the spirit and soul and discerns of the thoughts and intents of the heart. The sword has a hilt (handle) for you to but to rightly divide the word you need the mind of Christ. Christ chose his words, he gave you the words of life that God passed on to him. Your life depends on how you handle the word of God but you handle the word with your mind and spirit. Put God's word in your treasury and it will come out of your mouth as a sword.

God's word has the power to rebuke as it does to teach you how to live. God does not want you to keep his sword in its sheath but to use his sword to defend the hope that God has given you and give you the strength to stand against Satan's attack. God gave you a solid rock to build your house on so when the wind and rain come against you, you could stand.

Pray to stand firm.

Most of your trouble seems to come from the world and from those that God wants you to love. Paul tells you that you do not wage war with men but your fight is with the spirits that are at war with God. The weapons of men will not harm Satan thus, you have to fight a specific kind of war. This war of faith is not fought in this world or seen with your eyes but is in the heavens where God lives. You may have the sword of God but God fights this war in the heavens for you. Your part of this war is to let the sword of God come from your mouth trusting God to keep his promises.

There is no question that Satan wants to be god of all God has made. To Satan life is not holy and anything goes to make you serve him. Satan's plan is simple, you are in a war with evil that destroys everything in its path and Satan wants to take you as spoils of this war. Satan is not after you specifically but he wants to leave all God owns as charred remains. The weapons of any war are destructive and he will throw his darts at you to harm you. His fiery darts can influence your choices and bad choices take your life's work and destroy your life.

God's Son, who subdued the world, lives in you but the trials you face are smaller than he is. Take your doubts to God in prayer and cast your cares on him. Submit yourself to God and then rely on God for the help you need. You get stronger by thinking like God so meditate, make the time to be with God. Think about the trials others went through and look at the way things turn out. All the characters of the Bible stood in their time of trouble and they threw their cares on God. Some fasted while others fell on their knees and vented their frustration on the same God that cares for you. When you pray you must trust God to fulfill his word by standing on his word.

God is your partner in this war but the battle is won on your knees. Submit to God and let God crush the strong holds of Satan. When you cling to God's way of life and take a stand that resists evil, God will be with you. Your life is in God's hands and his hands is the refuge that will keep you safe.

God's test.

What do you look for when you go to the store to buy fruit? Do you look for peaches that are rosy and have the right feel? How the peaches look, feel, and smell tell you that the peaches are ready to eat. Your experience has told you how to test the peaches to know how they will taste before you take them home. In like manner, God has a test for you to see if you are truly his son.

God is testing your qualities to know that you are ready for his kingdom. God wants his child to mature with a strong and stable character that can face any trial that comes his way. The world is full of sin and God demands that you live as he does. God does not want you to change your mind or hope that trouble goes away but wants you to take a firm stand and show your faith in God. Using the qualities your father has taught you, you can go through the trial with a firm stand and still be right, just, and fair to all.

Some may study men to find out how to prosper but do you know what makes God prosper? God knows the power of the truth and he wants you to live by the truth. That truth will set you free to choose a positive plan that in the end will give you life in abundance. Your belief in God will make you firm but you too need to be like God who does not change.

CHAPTER 17

The Commitment To Be Effective

Worldly men achieve goals and are effective without God. They use the ideals and methods that God uses when it agrees with their own personal goals. Those that prosper know the value of a plan and the need to work it. They check from time to time the status of their plan and make changes that keep those goals. These men keep their goals in mind but God is not in their day to day life.

You are a part of God's future and it's a future with no end in sight. God will not force you to live up to his terms but wants you to serve him of your free will. When you make Jesus Lord of your life, God will give you a plan for you to live by. Everything you do from that moment on will stem from your love for God and his plan for your life.

God's main complaint with is the way man thinks and acts. For example, would God take a greasy hundred-dollar bill from your hand or would God prefer a crisp new bill? When you think of your life as that bill, would God want to touch you with his hands as long as you are that filthy? Its tough to handle grease with your hands without it getting it on the things you touch but your thoughts touch everything that comes in contact with you. God knows your thoughts but his plan is to clean your life up and shape how you think.

God wants you to forsake your own ways in exchange for the principles God wants you to use. The way you think and your behavior is on the top of your father's list. You may not think of God as your father but learning to yield and submit to God is vital to your new life. You may not see that God wants the best for you but you need a resolve to commit your life to do what God asks of you.

Learning new habits when the old ways are still fresh in your mind is hard to do. It is easier to keep the old habits than to cast then aside to learn new ones. The hardest time to change is right after you are born again and when sin is still a part of your habits. It seems as if you are on your knees asking God to forgive you for sin, more at that time than any other time of your life. The goal to keep from sinning is so tough that you may want to stop running the race. However, Jesus is in the race with you and is ready, willing, and able to get you back on your feet and in the race again. You need to remember that word to God does not have a stop clause, and giving your life to God is a commitment that you keep your eyes on to overcome the world.

Listen to your father who has a plan that will help you to manage your life. You have to decide how you are going to live and look for ways that you can do it. Be determined to manage your life with God's plan and work steadily for that goal. Take one day at a time and work with the idea that you're not going to quit just because things don't go your way. Don't settle for anything less than to get the job done, right.

Plans.

In your work place the plans are made by the executives and handed down to those who actually do the work. Then the plan is studied and the work is organized into steps that will make the plan feasible. By the time the work gets to the person who does the work, all one has to do is what you have been told to do. For you, God has passed his plans down to you and you have to use his plan and obey him. God has put his plan into steps that will help you to thrive and it is up to you to put his plan to work.

Plans give you a goal to work for but may not tell you how to do any of the work. House plans tell you where the outlets go, how the rooms are arranged, and where the sink goes. The plan does not tell you how to put the sink in or how to run the wire to the outlets. These plans work when you have the skills and the knowledge to do the work. However, most jobs begin with cleaning your work area of debris and moving the things that hinder you from doing the work. In doing the job you learn that things have to be done in an order so the work will go faster. When you have done your job, you need to look at what you did to make sure you did not leave parts out and make sure you did the job right.

Joshua 1:8-9 gives you a plan to make your life effective for both you and God. God's plan combines all the above to help you thrive and grow into the image of Christ. Do not let this Book of the Law depart from your mouth is part of the plan that you learn what God wants you to do. God's plan then tells you to "think about it day and night" that helps you to clear your mind from the debris and other things that hinder you from doing God's will. All of this is done so that you may do what is written in the book of the law. When the things that stop your work are out of the way, you can go to work and do your job. And when you have done your job right you will have success.

Show God your plan.

"Commit to the LORD whatever you do, and your plans will succeed." Prov 16:3. God wants to work with you so let God in on your plans. Plan to reach your goals by using godly methods and let God establish your plans. Take God to your job to show him what you plan to do and what you hope your work will do. Trust God to help you on your job and see what happens. Remember, commit your work to the Lord for without God you can do nothing.

Use proven methods.

Blue prints tell you what the house will look like when its done but they do not cover every detail you need to know. The prints tell you the materials to use and where you put them. The lumber does not jump off the truck or put them into place. Plans serve as a tool to achieve your goals and give you a general idea of what needs to be done. The details of the work are left for your personal touch. That means as long as the goal is reached that you can do the work the way you know to do the job.

All jobs start out at the entry level doing the grunt jobs that every one has to know. Plans call for specific things that need to be done but you also need to know what works and what don't. Proven ways come from doing the job many times and you need to use them since they are what you have to do to get the work done. After you know how to do the work then you can plan your day around the things you know will work.

God has a plan for your life that helps you to learn proven methods that will work for you. Starting out at the entry level you learn to work with his word and learn what his word is. Unlike those who gives you ten easy steps and then leaves, God stays with you to help you need to learn the ins and outs of his word. Then he put you into a position where you learn his ways so that you can prove his ways work. God wants you to know his plan and think about it so you can use it. When you have worked his plan in full, God has given you a promise that you will succeed.

God's way to be Effective.

God gave you additional promises to work with so you can take part in the plan of God. For example, the ideals you most admire about God are the grace he sheds on you. However, God's greatest desire is for you to shed his grace on the world. When the world sees you, God wants them to see what he looks like. By spending your time with God you begin to show his character and his fruit will flow from you.

Faith.

If you believe that God exists, and do little about it, would seem to be foolish. To please God you must believe that he exists and seek his face. David wrote. "Those who seek the Lord lack no good thing." Ps 34:10. "God rewards those who earnestly seek him." Heb 11:6. On the other hand, God sent the perfect gift to you in the form of Jesus Christ who came seeking the lost. Faith is more than trusting God and his son to serve your needs, you need to seek God to know him. Your trust in him gives you the, "I can do all things" attitude. On the other hand God has faith in you and knows what you are able to do.

God is not asking you, "what's in your pocket?" God is asking you to build your life in such a way that your life has the trust of others. The laws God asks you to obey are the things that you can do to build trust. He does not want you to lie, steal, or hurt people for the things you need in life, but to help them out. God does exactly what he said he would do and you need to keep your word so that others would have faith in you.

Goodness.

Did your mom ever tell you that you are good at being bad and bad at being good? You have a sense of what good is by what you want from others. Consider this, do you behave the way you want others to treat you? Good people are hard to come by and you can find faults in people if you want to. However, to be good, you have to make a choice to respect the sacredness of life. Everyone wants to be treated with respect and God wants you to make everyone feel needed.

Peter wrote. "Make every effort to add to your faith goodness." 2 Peter 1:5. It is a job for you to give 110% to God and have the best that life can give. Being right in the eyes of God is always within reach and you can excel when you live by God's word. You expect the best from others but by giving your best, you foster your own integrity. By giving 110% of your best to God, you will have the respect of others that you need in life.

Knowledge.

Knowledge is basic to any kind of life. You were born knowing only how to cry for your needs and from that day you learned how life worked. You built your life on the training you got from mom, dad and school, from there you went to college. Knowledge has a power you need for a good life but you had to work for it.

Solomon wrote Proverbs as if God himself was talking to his son. You can see the value that he put on his wisdom when talking to his son so that he would hear what he had to say. “My son, pay attention to what I say; listen closely to my words. Do not let them out of your sight, keep them within your heart; for they are life to those who find them and health to a man’s whole body.” Prov 4:20-22. You may wonder if Solomon went on to say, “The fear of the LORD is the beginning of knowledge, but fools despise wisdom and discipline.” Prov 1:7. Can you reflect back to the days when you were the child and you knew more than your parents did? Today your kids tell you that you are old and not living in today’s world. Now that you are older and, to some degree wiser, you have learned that your fathers word and his action was in your best interest. God wants to develop your thought life so you can think as an adult, holy and separated from evil.

God wants to, “Teach you that man does not live on bread alone but on every word that comes from the mouth of the LORD.” Deut 8:3. Knowledge comes from God’s mouth so you would have the help you need to make good choices. Since God is your father, he will not find fault in you but give you the wisdom you need. This does not mean that God wants you to be a clone but he wants you to show his way of life to others. God sheds his grace on you and he wants you to show his love to the world.

Self control.

God tells you, “In your anger do not sin.” Eph 4:26. To do this you must have control of your emotions. When you are angry you can let words fly that you regret you ever said. Being calm in the storms of life takes time to develop so do not burn bridges on your friends. God wants you to bring them to him.

Self control is a fruit of the Spirit that God gave you, therefore, learn to work with the spirit. Then you will have the mind to be calm and do what the holy life calls for. “Everyone who competes in the games goes into strict training. They do it to get a crown that will not last; but we do it to get a crown that will last forever.” 1 Cor 9:25. Obey the rules God gave you and learn to avoid evil. “Make every effort to be found spotless, blameless and at peace with him.” 2 Pet 3:14.

God has given you the choice to do anything you want to do. You can have as much fun as you want or you can make your choices based on what is best for your life. God has warned you ahead time that you are responsible for your choices. Take the time to think things out before you act on them.

Perseverance.

Perseverance is the work that you do to stay on the path to your goal. Work at a steady pace for the goal that you plan to achieve and know where you are at all times. Should you drift from the plan don’t fret, change what you are doing to get back on the path to your goals. Recommit to your original goal and make the things you do count, then keep your eye on the goal so that you are always running toward the goal.

The judge had to be tired of seeing the woman who wanted him to grant her justice but it was his job was to see that justice was served. For a long time judge ignored this woman but she just kept coming, saying, give me justice. She did God's will before, during and after the trial. She may have spent as much time on her knees crying out to God as she did in front of the judge. She kept going to the judge but she won her case with God before the judge gave his verdict. Can you see God behind the scenes, urging the Judge to grant the woman justice?

Godliness.

God lives on a higher plane than men do and his way of thinking exceeds our thoughts of what life is all about. God is a moral being that lives by the law of love and extends his grace to you. He lavishes his love on you with a desire to forgive you of your sins, even when you do not merit it. He makes things between you and him as if they had never happened. God wants to show his love for you no matter what you have done in your past.

Adopt God's way of life with a reverence for God. Hold his name as sacred giving him the respect that he asks for. Learn to love, forgive and give as

God does. Study the mind of God and take on the nature of God. God has found ways to make his life more productive but it is the relationship with you that he values most. Above all, treat others with respect knowing that they too, face the same kind of life you do. Keep this in mind, "There is not a righteous man on earth who does what is right and never sins." Eccl 7:20. Put your mind to the task and ask God for help you to be godly.

Kindness.

Kindness is your effort you make to brighten the day of others to cast a smile on your friends. It is the effort you make to help others with their work or help them with their coat. Kindness is what you take with you and the part of you that you leave to show your concern for others. Kindness is the thoughtful words that lift their spirits up or when you remember their birthday. Yet kindness may be as simple as crying when they are in pain and laughing with them when they are happy.

Kindness is being there to listen to them and not say a word. Being kind will bring your friends into your inner circle and lead them to your way of life. Friends have faults that either you overlook or bring out into the open. You may need to be forgiven by your friends so reckon that you have faults too. Be open and warm-hearted but give thought as to what you do because they have feelings that can be hurt.

Be humble.

One habit of successful men is that they seem to have time for friends and a need to make new friends. Friends help each other out and often their help has made you who you are today. You are important to God for he will make time for you and wants you for a friend. The question is, are you willing to be God's friend? Are you willing to tell God that you love him even when you make mistakes? Will you make time to change some of the things you do to keep God as a friend?

Being the low man on the seniority list has a good side as it helps you to know what God meant when he says to be humble. You have to treat others with respect since they have rank over you. God wants you to live in such a way that you live to serve the needs of others. Other people are worthier than you, when you are humble. Take stock of your life and lower yourself as Christ did. Christ had a lofty position in heaven but came to serve your needs as a ransom to free you from sin.

CHAPTER 18

Handling The Risks In Life

Courage is the manager of your skills that gives you the ability to face new areas of life with risks. You need courage to face life, rough times, conflict, and risks with a goal to succeed. Taking risks may hold you back or stop you cold but God has given you skills to do any job that he gives you. God will urge you to go and do but you have to muster the courage to use your skills for the work he has for you. You don't need courage for the job you know you can do, but it is for the job that has the risks you may fail at.

Life has so many risks that you can always find a reason to stop running the race. However, courage finds a way to run the race even when you feel it's no use to run any more. Satan tells you, "You can't" and God says he made you and knows you can do all things because he will give you the strength to do them.

Knowing what God has promised gives you the courage to stay in the race. God is your helper and he will give the strength that you need to stay in the race. The trust you have in God shows when you rely on God's help to run the race. What you know of God will help you to face anything that comes your way for you know that you can turn to God for help. However, that does not relieve you of the job or doing the work. All you need to know to have courage is that God is with you and with him you can do all things.

Courage does not get rid of rough times, the dangers or the risks of life. Instead you can face your trial knowing that God is with you and with his help you will overcome the world. Knowing that your stand in God is right helps when the world is busy making your life hard to live. They laugh at you, make fun of you, and reject your beliefs to discourage you. On the other hand, God's word says that Jesus Christ is all you need. His word feeds your spirit with power and truth no matter what comes your way. No matter what, you know that God will be there to help. All you need is the truth and the help of God when you take a stand against evil.

Courage is an asset that helps you to manage your skills and guide your life. It is not just for the times when you face a trial. You need to use your skills in the good times just to do your job. Your boss knows how to stretch your time and skills for his benefit? He will ask you to do more work than you think you can do. You also have times that your trials are so big that you think that you can't handle it. You seem to be OK when you face things that you can see, but what of the danger you can not see? The conflict you have with evil is one area of your life that you can not pass the buck. God wants you to manage your skills in those gray areas as well.

When Satan attacks you, you can't say that's not my job or try to find a place to hide. You can't run from him and Satan won't go away unless you resist him. Satan attack is so real that you need the courage of God to resist him. God is with you 24 hours every day of the year whether its good times or the bad times of your life. In thick and in thin God is a source of strength that is ready to help you when you need him. If anything, God gives you a reason to submit yourself to him and his grace.

Godly Courage.

God wants you to give him the best you can give and frankly expects you to use the skills he has given you. God knows that you can obey him since he has done all he can to help you deal with the reasons why you can't. When God gives you an assignment he expects you to do it because he made you and knows what you are able to do. Now it is up to you to perform, but remember this, Christ sent the disciples out in pairs of two. There is nothing magical with the help of a like mind person to build your courage.

The problem comes when you can't see the stuff that Satan is doing in his realm. Satan sneaks up on you and gives you the reasons to sit it out and park it on the bench. Sitting this one out may seem like a good choice when you can feel danger, but what if you see nothing that tells you that you are in harms way. At the same time you feel the weight of the world on your shoulders and its all going to come crashing down on you. What do you do? You know what God has asked you to do. Satan knows that if you had the courage to do the job you would be on top of the world. When Satan has his way he will drain you of your courage so he can keep you on the bench.

You need God's word to calm the sea of choices that is tossing you every which way but loose. Doing things in a state of panic will cause you to do things that may cost you your life. You are in charge of the way you think and what you do. You need to be calm and use your head in times that tempt you to make irrational choices.

When you goof up on the job, your boss will tell you to keep your mind on the job. Your boss expects you to use your mind to do his work but you need to keep your eyes on Christ. Your boss robs you of the right to think on God's word. However, Satan is also good at taking your mind off your goals and in place, put your trials where that's all you see. It takes an informed mind to know the truth and how to use the truth to resist Satan. You may not have the time to think about options when your trial hits but being prepared to stand in God makes good sense.

Make it a habit to read and study the Bible that prepares you for the day of the trial.

Managing your feelings.

Feelings that can be seen on your face reflect the way you are thinking but the reasons for your feelings can not be seen with your eyes. How you feel may be what a friend did or what they said that affects you. What they say can lift you up or it will find home port where ill feelings will drop anchor in your soul. What others say and do shape the reasons that foster the feelings you have for them. You may want to keep the good feelings but you have to shed the bad feelings as they affect the way you think. One of the better things you can do is to learn to manage how you feel.

Your feelings can justify what you do and let you give evil for evil. God wants you to stop the process of evil and do good things in return for the evil you receive. What they did to you is no reason to get even but a way for you to be evil. "Do not be deceived: God cannot be mocked. A man reaps what he sows." Gal 6:7. Still, God wants you to obey him and in doing so you will sow the seed of a godly life.

Your feelings let you assume that they are guilty without a trial. You have had thoughts that are based on what has occurred to you or on what you have seen and heard. In your own mind you think from your side of the issue and make a good case for the guilt of others. You clearly have not done a thing wrong but taken the liberty to assume the worst. Then you cast the blame on others, without taking the time to ask questions. "When you, a mere man, pass judgment on them and yet do the same things, do you think you will escape God's judgment?" Rom 2:3. God has asked you not to judge or take things as true without proof. God wants you to, "Test everything. Hold on to the good. Avoid every kind of evil." 1Thes 5:21-22.

The sense of feeling tells you the size and shape of things around you. They give you a sense of bearing and let you know where you stand. Feelings control your emotions and you have learned to trust those feelings to guide your life. Your five senses guide your life but what gives you the feeling of being harmed when there is nothing in our sight to fear? Lets remember that you are also a spirit being with senses that work in God's realm. "They have eyes to see but do not see and ears to hear but do not hear, for they are a rebellious people." Ezek 12:2.

God says you have ears that hear and eyes that see in the spirit world but you don't use because all you can see is the things in the world. "The god of this age has blinded the minds of unbelievers, so that they cannot see the light of the gospel of the glory of Christ, who is the image of God." 2 Cor 4:4. God wants you to use the eyes he gave you and will open your eyes so you may see into the spirit realm.

The Bible tells you that Satan exists and that he is a lion out to have you for lunch. Satan crouches at your door and when you open it he is ready to pounce. (Paraphrase Gen 4:7). The Bible also says, "Do not give the devil a foothold." Eph 4:27. That means you should have a healthy respect for Satan. Even though you can't see him with human eyes, you know that he is lurking about. Evil is so strong that it can be felt and reacted to. You feel the presence of God when you go to Church but you may not be aware that you can feel the presence of evil. Your feelings tell you that you are in the presence of good and evil. Your feelings may be your spiritual eyes and ears into the spirit realm. Your feelings will urge you to take a step of faith and they will make you shrink from doing God's will.

The sense of fear and danger tell you that you can be hurt if you don't take action now. Courage allows you to live in a godly manner in spite of how you feel and it finds a way for you to face the trial. Courage is the inner motives that drive you to do the job with the power of your mind. Your spirit and mind draws on Jesus for the strength you need to live for, "Without Jesus you can do nothing." John 15:5. When you learn to rely on God you learn that, "I can do all things through Christ which strengtheneth me." Phil 4:13(KJV) God supports your life with encouragement and keeping Phil 4:13 in your mind will help you face the risk of life. Fear can rule your mind or you seek God through his word for the strength you need. God has given you the choice to live in fear or with his help live by faith. You will face risks every day of your life but you will have a better life when you face every risks with God's help. Fear has the power to rule your life but courage puts your fear aside so you can be productive.

The Use of your faith.

When you read your Bible, you will hear words like these. "All things are possible with God." Mk 10:27. "Apart from Christ I can do nothing." John 15:5. "So then faith cometh by hearing, and hearing by the word of God. "Rom 10:17(KJV) Listen to his word because God will encourage you to lean on him to fight the battle.

Satan is not stupid but he has learned his skills from God and is not afraid to come at you all out. He has nothing to lose by lying to you and more to gain should you fall into his trap. He has an influence on you and is bold enough to suggest what you should do. This is why you need to read his profile in God's word to know how to resist him.

God's word gives you the courage you need at the time you need it. God is your risk cutter because he gives you the courage and the truth to be productive. You can do anything you put your mind to do when you work with God. God is the source of your strength and he goes to work in the spirit realm to make your plans come together. Working with God adds strength to your skills for God will add his to yours. "Let us then approach the throne of grace with confidence, so that we may receive mercy and find grace to help us in our time of need." Heb 4:16. The next time your feelings tell you to hide show them the power of God's word.

A gambler will bet all he has on a sure thing since the return will give him the faith to risk all he has. You need that kind of return too and you have it when you put your trust in God's word. God gave you a plan to follow and a sure way to obtain eternal life. You need to show the courage God has given you to stand up to the intimidation of evil. Jesus said that the kingdom of God is like a man who found a pearl with high value in a field. That man knew the value of the pearl and he sold all he had to buy that field. God is asking that you have the courage to give or sell all you have to for a sure thing.

Can You Trust God?

No one in power likes the attitude of doubt for it is the mindset that says, "It can't be done." You have a job to do for God but doubt gives you a vision of that it can't be done. No one wants to fail but faith gives you a vision of the finished job. The attitude of doubt kills the success of any job and keeps you from making plans.

Jesus said, "With God all things are possible." Matt. 19:26. God makes what you do for him, feasible because you have your part to do and God has his part. Don't be afraid to ask for God's help since your faith relies on Christ doing the job that he agreed to do. Your faith in God will give you the courage to rely on Christ and to place your trust in God. Pray before you do any work for God and let him know that you are relying on him for his help. When you rely on God you will not be alone for he will be with you.

Overcoming Satan.

God wants you to fan your coals until they burst into a flame but Satan wants to put your fire for God out. Satan wants to stop you from doing things God's way and halt your desire to trust in God. His goal is to make you fall from God's grace and to make you his slave. To do that he will make every step of yours hard. Satan wants you to conform to the way the world thinks and to be like those he controls. Satan knows that when you do not obey God, you will lose your strength. That makes God's stand harder to achieve so he can have his way with you. Your faith in God gives you an attitude that you can do it and that attitude will heap coals of fire on Satan.

Satan is persistent and he will wear you to a frazzle. That is the moment that your tempers flare up and you are ready to give birth to sin. People tend to say that is enough when they are beaten to a pulp. Satan wants you to fill your time up with fun or so much pain that so you won't take life serious and keep you too busy to pay attention to God. Then you ask what happened when the roof falls in. However, you have 24 hours in the day to fill and you won't stop living when you are tired of the stumbling blocks Satan puts in your path. Satan has the most to lose if you were to do God's will. He will come to you as he did to Eve to give you his side of the story. Keep this in mind, Satan is a liar that can sell a freezer to an Eskimo and that you can be deceived by his lies. The best way to overcome Satan is to know the truth but to know the truth about God so spend time in God's word.

The Courage to be a friend.

Saying you want no part when your friends are about to sin takes courage. Having friends is a source of strength that you can enjoy. The fear of losing them as friend begs you to join in their fun but compromise is one way you fall into sin.

Not long ago, a friend of mine was asked to read the palm of an acquaintance. When my friend agreed, I got up and started to leave. She said that I did not have to leave. In reply I said, you know what you are doing is wrong. I left her and later that night she saw me and sat down with me to talk. She assumed that I was playing the role of God and that my conduct troubled her. Her feelings told her that she was going to lose a friend but I had to reassure her that it was not her, but the sin that I ran from. My courage to avoid sin gave me a chance to witness to her even though she has not changed her mind. We still are friends and she still read palms but now she comes to me for godly advice.

As it turned out, my friend did not want to lose me as a friend. Yet she was playing with sin that I wanted no part of. She needed to know that God does not want her to perish but to be saved through Jesus Christ. I confronted her with my beliefs and the choice that God gives to every man. I wish that I could make that choice for her for God has a use for a sweet person like her.

Friends will not hurt you on purpose but it takes courage to confront the issues that you want no part of. Let all your friends know that you walk with Christ and your father does not want you to do those things. Tell your friends that God will accept them as they are and you will too. Use your courage to be up front with your friends and you will gain their respect.

Making it a choice.

Joshua 1:9 tells you that God has commanded you to be strong and courageous. This is not an option to Christian life but an ability God has given to you. Success is a result of hard work and the goals you achieve come from a plan. Success does not come to those who wait for it but to those who make the choice and have the resolve to work for goals. Without a resolve to work the plan, you will have little to show for your work.

Resolve is the spirit that you will do what it takes to do all that is written in the law. Courage is the sister to resolve and she finds a way to do all that is written in the law. Courage and resolve work hand in hand with your goals. Your will drives you to do what God has commanded you to do but you have to do the work. The job that God gives you will take you into enemy territory where you have to tell the good news. The word of God may not be taken well but you still have a job to do for God. While you are doing the job for God, Satan will attack you. He will try to stop you but you have to muster the courage to do God's will.

Courage helps you find your strengths and ways to use them. Your life is always under attack because Satan is out to take your testimony. You are God's diplomat to the world and it is your job to take the word of God to the world. The way you take God's word to the world makes the difference, and as a Christian, your courage will be tested. The resolve to do the will of God will put your courage to work, but you have to make the choice to serve God at any cost.

Courage of Christ.

Jesus was driven to do the will of God, even at the cost of his life. His attitude was to do the will of God no matter what. "My food," said Jesus, "is to do the will of him who sent me and to finish his work." John 4:34. Christ wanted to do the will of God and nourished his life by doing the work that God sent him to do. God showed his love for you when Jesus laid on the cross and let others nail his body to it.

CHAPTER 19

Paralyzed By What May Happen

> "Do not be terrified; do not be discouraged"
>
> Joshua 1:9.

Let's look back to the 11th of September 2001 when for the first time America saw what terror could do. Those who live in New York can say that they were not in the towers when the passenger planes struck. In the days that followed 911, all you could think of was that you could have been there. You learned that a few fanatics went to extremes to tell you to listen to their woes. You saw that men from the other side of the world could kill you but they also took some of the freedoms that you have had all your life. Today, the belief that this could happen again limits what you can do to be safe. Those that want to force their way of life on you have a grasp on you with terror.

Life goes on and for now, New York is going back to the way it was. The shock of terror is over but your life has changed with the events of 9-11. Today your time is spent learning how to be safe in the future. Terror is an act of criminals that have no morals and those who intimidate you with the use of threats to rule your life. They use the thought that you or your family could be hurt unless you do what they want. Just as terror has gripped our nation with the fear of flying, Satan uses terror to sap your strength to keep you from doing things, as God wants you to.

Fear that is built in man.

My wife shrieks when a tick is on her. She screams out in panic because she is afraid to touch the tick already on her. All she can say is, "Get this tick off me!" On the other hand, what if a friend was to nudge you as a joke while you are leaning over the edge of a cliff? Wouldn't you give, ten easy safety lessons to the one that pushed you and tell them that you could have been killed?

Feelings are normal to this kind of stimulus for you were in danger or harms way. The tick bite has the potential to make you sick and you knew that falling from the cliff to the ground would kill. In both cases, your senses told you that you were in harms way. Your instinct to live set off an alarm in your mind and it told you that you had to take steps to be safe.

Fear takes a toll on your heart, making it beat so

hard that you can hear it. God gave you fear for a reason but fear affects what you do. Being afraid has saved you from harm in the past but fear has made you tremble and scared the wits out of you. Most of the time you react to fear without taking the time to think because you trust and listen to the feeling fear gives you.

Is there a safe way?

Today man takes time to study accidents for the cause and designs a way to make the things you work with safe. As a result, the tools that you use in your work place and in your homes are safer. Today the workplace trains you to be safe and the use of seat belts is a law in your state. Life is such that no one wants to go home with less than they went to work with.

Human error is still the main cause of accidents and why most safety rules get bent. People think that they are smarter than the machine or want to beat the system. You can be taught how to be safe but they can not make you obey the rules. Most men still do things their way, which carries over into their spiritual life. Here they assume that if they are good they will go to heaven or they have a way to get to Heaven without God. People that try to beat God's system assume more than they should and will get hurt.

God has a plan for you to go to heaven and by taking his plan to heart that you will arrive safely. You have a choice to make for your life relies on using God's plan. Take time to think, aren't your ways always right until you get hurt. Without God's plan you are going to get hurt by bending the rules or not reading them at all. Your ego will not let you admit that you were wrong but then it is too late to change what you have done? Then too, you may know the plan of Salvation but not do anything about it. God has a plan for those who refuse to repent and his verdict is final. The Bible says this of God's plan, "The LORD works out everything for his own ends— even the wicked for a day of disaster. The LORD detests all the proud of heart. Be sure of this: They will not go unpunished." Prov 16:4-5.

Do you have the fear of God? The fear of God is different from the terror that Satan uses to control you. You have been given a respect of God to know that he will do what he says he will do but Satan uses lies to scare you out of your wits. All you can see is the harm that may happen to you and the way you react benefits Satan more than it does God. The fear of God is a respect for what God can and will do. Your respect for God makes the time to listen to the rules and let's you heed the warnings that God gives to every man.

Satan's use of terror.

Not long ago I was going to see a lady in the county home just outside town. By the time I got to the car I felt something bad was going to happen. I also had five reasons why I should not go, which left me in a dilemma, should I stay home. The feelings I had were stronger for staying. I am sure same kind of thing occurs to others but I questioned why I felt fear. When I had visited her before she clung to me as I left. I wanted to see this lady because she was spending her last days in a county home. I loved her and had the reasons to go, but why did I fear going? She's left this world to be with the Lord shortly after this test of mine and I am sorry I did not go to see her.

Terror is an art to Satan and he wants you to be so timid that you will be afraid to do God's will. You are not in a war with men but with evil and those who use evil to lie, steal, and kill. You have to deal with Satan's tactics since he will attack the way you think just for taking the gospel to men. It is all a lie. How can Satan harm you when you are in God's hand? The odds are that you will not see the proof of those fears when you do the will of God. However, you will know the joy of doing God's will unless you go to work.

Feelings play an important role in my life since I felt led to step out in faith to write this book. God has impressed his needs on me and I could hear what as going on in the spirit realm. This fact started questions running through my mind if Satan could do the same things. If anything, the roar of a lion would get my attention and I felt Satan roar many times. At times I wonder because of the way I balked when deciding to go the will of God. Could I feel the presence of Satan though my eyes could not? Then I wondered. How could so many in the church say they felt the presence of the Lord when I had not? I was left to conclude that those in the spirit realm can lead you by your feelings.

Where do the reasons come from that let you put God off? What makes you shy away from doing the will of God? From my experience I know that the reasons why, I can't do God's will, have flooded my mind in the past. I know that I want to do God's will but when I feel the fear of harm I stop. I stop even when God says do not be afraid.

"For what I do is not the good I want to do; no, the evil I do not want to do— this I keep on doing." Rom 7:19. We are all in this boat but Satan has you walking on pins and needles. You are in a war that goes on in the spirit realm but that war affects what you do. It is a war of faith fought over the way you think and act and your trust in the truth. Satan tries to replace the "I can do it attitude" with doubt and fear of harm but you can't let him do it.

The terror of Satan is a stimulus that tells you to shrink back. His work is like the sound of the whip that forces a slave to do the will of its master. Satan is the model slave owner. He knows that the crack of the whip does as much as the sting and he will take you to the edge of the top floor to push you off. He just wants to keep your life in turmoil and chaos, so he can take you to his den. Terror breaks the will to resist and causes you to find safety before you can use your mind to think. The fear of harm can paralyze and stifle your ability to do God's will. "Submit yourselves, then, to God. Resist the devil, and he will flee from you." James 4:7.

Who is at blame?

Satan is filled with rage. Rage is a form of anger that builds, to the point that it explodes. Do you like to be near angry people? Does being in the same room with those who show their anger make you cringe? With this feeling, all you want to do is get out of their way.

There are some that feel that Satan is the reason that everything goes wrong. He may be a pest but when things go bad he is easy to blame. You can say the devil made me do it.

Oh, Come on now!

You can see a demon behind every nook and cranny. The demons are the blame for the very things you did and went wrong. It seems that you have the right answer to shed the blame for what you have done or at least, that is the way you want to see life. You didn't do anything wrong but now you have someone or something to blame for your actions.

God is not behind everything you do because God gave you a mind of your own so you alone make the choices that affect your life. God will not tempt you to sin and you can not blame him for your sin. God asks that you resist Satan and that alone should tell you that Satan exists. Then God spoke of Satan's pride, his sin, and of his skill to lie. Whether you make the choice for life or not God wants you to know that your are liable for the choices you make. The all knowing God knows why you fail to run the race right. "My people are destroyed from lack of knowledge." Hosea 4:6. "They perish because they refused to love the truth and so be saved." II Th 2:10. No one can make you do anything and you have no one to blame but yourself. Thus it may be wise to take God to heart.

How do I resist?

Paul says that the saints do not wage a war as men do. A spiritual war is alien to the men of this world and is not fought on the same terms that men use. This war is going on in the spirit realm where God and Satan live. God clearly won the war in heaven and when the war was over, God cast Satan out of heaven down to earth. Stripped of a way to fight a war with God, Satan is after the apple of God's eye. That's you. Man knows more about what he can see, touch and feel than he does about the spirit realm. In this realm, man has to deal with life and death of another kind. Here, man must trust God to fight the war with evil or die with sin.

Feeling that rule your emotion affects the way your mind thinks, and the choices it makes. Feelings tell you how to think and act but what if, your thoughts and feelings could be manipulated from an out side source and you don't know it? The war in your spirit is waged over good and evil but the old man is so familiar with this war that he doesn't pay attention to it. God wants you to renew your mind so you can prove what is right or wrong in his eye. God's word will open your eyes to the spirit realm so you know what to do.

Meditating or thinking on God's word is a way that you can think like God. Paul said something to this effect, do not conform to the world but renew the way your mind thinks. You can know the will of God and be able to prove it. Those who are mature, use God's word to live and are trained to distinguish good from evil. You need to spend time in God's word and put it in your heart so you can take it with you wherever you go. You will never know when you will be tempted but having the mind of Christ will help you to see evil when it shows up. Satan will force a choice on you so you will do things his way. However, it is a choice on your part to shun evil and resist its influence.

When fear strikes.

What terror does is short circuit the way you think since it blows the fuses in your mind. With a blown fuse you react from instinct and do things the way Satan leads you. Isaiah said. "You will keep in perfect peace him whose mind is steadfast, because he trusts in you." Isa 26:3. Those who hold fast to God and his word have peace of mind. When your mind is at peace there is no fear and that gives you the time to think. Learning from God's word is like replacing the blown fuse with a fuse that can take the surge of Satan's influence.

Do not be dismayed because God does not want you to lose your courage in the face of danger. Should you dread doing God's work, the work will not get done. The dread of doing a job will throw your commitment to God out the window. The trouble is that you will not know that you were dismayed, but if anything, dread tells you that you are in the line of fire. Losing your desire to serve God is a signal that you need to get back into his word. You need the courage to fight back in faith and you need to run to God for help. God can do more than you can think or imagine according to the power that is in you (Eph 3:20). Satan does not want you to release the power of God that lives in you. No one should be afraid to do God's will. The joy of doing God's will is hard to explain but you lose that joy when you allow fear to dictate what you do for the Lord.

"For God did not give you a spirit of timidity, but a spirit of power, of love and of self-discipline." 2 Tim 1:7. Being timid robs you of your confidence and makes you hesitate. Paul goes on to say, "So do not be afraid to share the Lord with others." "Join with me by the power of God to do the work God has called me to do." 2Tim 1:8. Guard the spirit that God has given you and put the word of God that gives you courage in your heart.

Keeping your mind on the job is not easy when a bucket of ice water is thrown on you. Just as sudden, fear robs you of your strength to serve God. Both ice water and fear will stop you in the midst of your work until you regain your senses. Fear makes you focus on your needs and takes your mind off God. God wants the best you can give but living in fear will paralyze your spirit.

CHAPTER 20

God Is With You 24—7

> How will anyone know that you are pleased with me and with your people unless you go with us? What else will distinguish me and your people from all the other people on the face of the earth?" And the LORD said to Moses, "I will do the very thing you have asked, because I am pleased with you and I know you by name."
>
> Exodus 33:16 - 17.

God is a friend!

One thing is certain that God is beyond understanding and it would take more than a lifetime to know God. You can spend a your life in God's word, in prayer and thinking about his word just to know

God. Think of it, God is with you 24 hours 7 days a week and he will be with you till the day he comes for you. The best thing that you can do is to make time for God and be available to him at anytime of the day.

God has made a commitment to you that you would never be alone. God will be with you no matter where you go or what you do because you are precious to him. God knows you and he will set you apart from the world as someone special. God does not want you to perish and all he asks is that you obey him. When you asked Christ into your life, God adopted you and became your father. As your human father would do, your father in heaven will help you to grow up. He's there to pick you up, fix you up and to send you on your way. God wants to be a part of your life and a father who protects you from harm. He will take you by the hand and lead you to new places. He's interested in what you are doing and wants to help you to do what is right in his sight.

Have you ever wished that you had paid more attention to what your father said? Have you learned from hindsight that he knew more than you did? You had to learn everything the hard way and you were in hot water most of the time. Your father built a relationship that you will have as long as you live and no matter what you do he will always be your father. Nothing can change that, but fail to see him for five to ten years and you will drift away from him. The warmth of your relation will grow cold just as your love for God will go with the lack of time spent with him.

God wants to be at your side.

There may have been a time when you stuck your finger in God's face and said, leave me alone, go away. Your heart was stained with sin and you saw no need for God. Later on in life you had to ask, why would a Holy God want any part me?

You may not have known that you were sinning and grieving the God that wants to give you a gift of life. God so loved you that while you were deep in sin, Christ paid the price of your sin. He let men nail him to a cross and then lift him up so the whole world could see him die a horrible death. He died to save you from a death worse than his but God asked Jesus to bear your sins on the cross for you. When you take Jesus as your savior you accept the death of Christ as the penalty for your sin as if it was paid in full. His blood was the price God asked for, in other words God forgave you, and your sins are now history. In God's sight you are holy and he came to live in you.

Your Father wants you to do all that he has written in the book of law. To help you work his plan, God will be at your side. Your father wants you to have the best that you are capable of being and is in you to give the help that you need it. God knows how to prosper and the things you need to do to have a successful life.

God will work with you as long as it takes and as much as you let him. God will show you how to be creative by doing his will, he will give you on hands training and give you a goal to work for. God has a plan for you that will fit your life and he will help you reach those goals. Prospering boils down to a few words that only God can say, "Well done, my good servant!" Luke 19:17.

The help I need.

"Where can I go from your Spirit? Where can I flee from your presence? If I go up to the heavens, you are there; if I make my bed in the depths, you are there." Ps 139:7-8. The psalmist wrote the idea that we do not always see. He asks, can I flee from your presence but both the Father and the Son has promised to be with you. So you can go beyond Pluto or to the darkest places in Africa and God will be with you.

The Bible says that God walked in the cool of the day with Adam. However one day, Adam must have looked strange to God since he had covered his body with fig leaves. God asked, how did you know you were naked? Have you eaten from the tree I told you not to eat from? Sin had changed how God saw man for Adam knew he was naked and he had tried his best to cover his sin, the only way he knew how.

God knew that man could not deal with his sin in his own way. Sin affects both the injured party and the one that sinned. Sin does not choose the place of birth but it is the heart of man that gives birth to sin. No matter the size or kind of sin, sin will become a weed and the only way to deal with sin is God's way. Your sin has to be pulled as if it was a weed and cast aside.

Adam and Eve chose to cover their nakedness

with fig leaves. In a similar way, man has tried to cover his sin in his own way. Their leaves had to be drying and cracking with time, which exposed their sin. Like Adam, even the sin that you try to cover will find you out. In time Adam would have to hide the sin that made its way through the leaves. Sin will come back to haunt you and only God could come up with a better solution for sin. In Genesis, God went to Adam in the cool of the evening and assessed the condition of Adam and Eve. God knew what to do and went and prepared garments Adam and Eve out of skins. The skins tell you that something gave its life for the atonement for sin. The blood was shed for man's was a shadow of God's plan to deal with the sins of man in the future.

Where would man be if it were not for God? God does not want you or those near you to perish but sin will affect everyone's life. Though God is sinless, God wants you to know that your sin hurts him. God does not want to lose you as a friend, but that sin drives him out of your life. God is the first to confront your sin and lets you know that he sees your faults. Then he offers a way to turn from sin and make things right with him. If it were not for God man would be in a helpless state. God has made a way the sin of man would not make him hostile towards man and sent his son the atonement of man's sin.

The assurance of God.

Your body is a temple, a sacred place that God dwells in by his spirit. God marks his children with a seal the Holy Spirit who leads his sons to a holy life. This seal is placed on you to say that you belong to God with the promise of what is to come. (2 Cor 1:21-22.) The Holy Spirit is the promise that God gives to help you stand firm in Christ. He is God's down payment of what is to come and has set you aside for the day he comes for you. Stores have a method that you buy things on lay away. You put some of your cash down on the things you want and they hold them till you can pay for them. God gave you his Holy Spirit as a pledge at the layaway counter of life, saying that on the day he returns, you will be one of those he takes to heaven.

Created to be one.

At the time of creation God said, "It is not good for the man to be alone." Gen 2:18. God then put Adam into a deep sleep and took a rib from him and from that rib God made a helper for Adam. God wanted man to dwell on the earth and God made a helper for man to be at his side. Apart the two could not obey God's first command to go and fill the earth and the two had to work as a team to conceive. In addition, God called Adam and Eve by the same name. Could it be, did God call them Mr. and Mrs. Adam? Gen 5:2 KJV. Nevertheless, God's plan was for man to unite and become one flesh.

God wants to unite with you but he is a spirit. Your spirit is bound inside your body looking out and God is in your body and in your heart. To explain Jesus said, "On that day you will realize that I am in my Father, and you are in me, and I am in you." John 14:20. When God adopts you as his own child, he gives you his Spirit that leads you wherever he goes.

> "Two are better than one, because they have a good return for their work: If one falls down, his friend can help him up. But pity the man who falls and has no one to help him up! Also, if two lie down together, they will keep warm. But how can one keep warm alone? Though one may be overpowered, two can defend themselves. A cord of three strands is not quickly broken."
>
> Eccl 4:9-12.

One strand can snap easily but having more strands will make you stronger. God sends his spirit into of you to bear fruit but you need to agree to work as a team with him. Two are better than one, as Eccl 4:9-12 states you gain strength from team effort. God knows that apart from God you can do nothing and that you are the branch that is joined to the vine and pruned by the father. God prunes sin from your life so you may bear more fruit. God has a plan to see that you prosper and a plan to give you hope and a future and he is eager for you to see your future with your own eyes.

God makes a commitment to you.

"I have given them the glory that you gave me, that they may be one as we are one." John 17:22. In this prayer, Jesus shows you that he did not plan for you to be alone. If anything, his plan for you is to partake of the divine nature through his promises. God wants to guide you into the truth so he can remind you of what he has said. God is in you to help when you need him because God does not want you to lose out on life. Alone you have no power to do all God expects of you and God is the edge you need to do all that is written in his word. With his help you can do all he has asked and since God watches over his word, he will do exactly what he said he would do.

"Greater is he who is in you than he that is in the world." 1 Jn. 4:4. Look at how the world lives and you will know that you need the power of God to keep you from sin. The world wants to have the clout and the money that puts the world on easy street. It's a dog eat dog world because of the way they live. The God who is in you makes a distinction in who you are and lets you stand out from the world.

God's standards are tough to live up to but you have the power of God in you to lean on. God lives in me so, "I can do all things through Christ Jesus who strengthens me." Phil 4:13. "Do two walk together unless they have agreed to do so?" Jesus said, "I am the way and the truth and the life." John 14:6. "I will be with to the end of the age." Matt. 28:20. Jesus has made a commitment to you and he has made these promises so you can own the prize at the end of the race. For everything that was written in the past was written to teach us, so that through endurance and the encouragement of the Scriptures we might have hope. Rom 15:4

Working as one.

The idea that two people could be one flesh was an idea that was hard to understand. Being one flesh is a way that the male and female conceive. You need a meeting of the minds from both sides to agree before you to join with your one and only. The same rule applies to God. When God is speaking of being one with you he is speaking of a face to face, personal relationship with your spirit. Therefore, God has a feasible plan that the two of you need to agree on before the goals that both of you want can be achieved. God offers a plan that will build you into a man that is worthy of eternal life. However, you have to take part in his plan before the day of decision when all men come before him.

CHAPTER 21

Talking To Your Heavenly Father

Prayer is when you spend your time to tell God how you feel, what your hopes are and what you need. Your Heavenly Father will listen to you and give you the good things that you need. Prayer lets you see God as a friend and that you can cast your cares on him. God is so trustworthy that you can share your deepest secrets with and know that they are safe.

God is himself when he speaks to you so it is a good idea to be yourself when you talk to him. You don't need a set routine or special way to pray to God and get answers because short prayers like "help" work too. You don't have to pretend with God or make a big show to impress your father. Giving him the straight truth works wonders.

Can you talk to God if you are afraid of offending

him? The Bible says this, "For we do not have a high priest who is unable to sympathize with our weaknesses, but we have one who has been tempted in every way, just as we are— yet was without sin. Let us then approach the throne of grace with confidence, so that we may receive mercy and find grace to help us in our time of need." Heb 4:15-16. Jesus went through the fire having been tempted as you are and have faced the trials you have. In addition, God is with you 24-7 and he knows that your life doesn't have a bed of roses. He knows that you are not perfect and that you have faults. However, it is hard to offend God when you treat him with respect and honor his place in your life.

God loves you and wants to hear from you. God is a busy person but not so busy that he won't make the time to hear what you have to say. On the other hand, stretching out your prayers may put God's hand under his chin and he may yawn of sheer boredom. The object of prayer is to make your needs clear to God but the length of prayer may confuse exactly what you want. It's how great God is, but when you lengthen your prayer, God may wonder how great you art. It is better to tell God your needs than it is to make prayers that mean nothing or are a show for people to see.

How do you speak to God?

Prayer is one topic that many men write about and all agree, prayer works. Everyone has his own ideas on what prayer is and how to pray. Yet you are one of a kind and what works for one man may not work for you. One man tells the story of his life and another man says little if he talks at all. Your prayer needs to fit your character so be true to God. Pray in a fashion that you are at ease when you talk to your Father. You don't have to feel godly to talk to God.

Have you asked your father for the keys to the car or did you beg for the keys? Did you give him the respect that he demanded of you and promised the car back without dents? Did you address him the way he wants or did you call him by his first name? Did you add the magic word, please? You knew what your father demanded and did what you had to do to get those keys. Do you know God demands that you give him the dignity he deserves?

You need to consider that wants are the toys that use up your time and keep you from your work. Needs are the shoes that cover your feet, food on the table and your father's advice. Can you tell him why you need the things you ask for? Talking to your father is vital but remember this, God will not refuse to give you the things you need. You just need to give your father reasons that your needs are for your well being and tell him in a way that he can agree with you.

How does God speak to you?

God speaks from a position of supreme authority and when God commands, you know what you have to do. He has the authority to tell you what to do and where to go. He has the right to raise you to be an adult by his standards. God speaks directly at the issue he is dealing with and is blunt in how he says it. God says that, "All have sinned and fall short of the glory of God." Rom 3:23. God is frank but clear when he speaks and that means there is no way around it, you have sinned. Study his skills of speech and you will be effective in what you ask God for.

Praying with dignity.

You pray because God exists, and you have put your trust in him for the things that you need. You may pray to any god for the things you need but will you ask God for your needs again if he does not reply? Only morons would say you might as well be speaking into the air than to pray to God. If prayer is polluting the air with your words, then why do you pray? Your prayer has a clear goal hoping that God will respond to your needs. You ask God for your needs with the faith that you will get them. When God answers your prayer, you know that he exists and he knows you.

On the other hand, why must we pray to a God that already knows what you need? The answer is right on the front of your face and you may not want him to stick his nose into your affairs? God moves by a grace that gives you dignity and the respect you need. The point is this, until you have a need and make that request known to God. God will not interfere in your life but when you ready to ask him, he is open to serve your needs.

Can you blame God if you fail to ask for what you need? God's habit is to wait on you so you may ask for your needs and that practice gives you the dignity of a choice. If God were to give you what you want and were to do things for you before you asked for them, would you have a reason to talk to him? There could be a point in time that you may resent all the things he does for you. The choice to call on God is voluntary and the way God replies to your need shows his love for you. The troubles the world hands out, are enough to put any man on his knees to seek God for help. Prayer is a voluntary act of worship but God gives you the right and the dignity to ask him for help in your time of need.

Honor your father.

Christ went off to be alone away from men just to be with God. God's word tells you that Christ had a strong prayer life. Though the Bible does not reveal all of Christ's prayers, his word says. "During the days of Jesus' life on earth, he offered up prayers and petitions with loud cries and tears to the one who could save him from death, and he was heard because of his reverent submission. Although he was a son, he learned obedience from what he suffered." Heb 5:7-8.

God's word gives Christ humanity by saying that he suffered emotionally and his prayers were filled with passion. He had a heart for man, so much that he wept when his friend Lazarus, died. He went to his grave and cried out to God in agony to raise

Lazarus from the dead. The tone of Jesus' voice spoke of a man who cared about how his friends felt over the loss of their brother.

Still, Christ was devoted to God, during his life, as a boy he said to his mother and father. "Didn't you know I had to be in my Father's house?" Luke 2:49. Just before his death he said. "My food," said Jesus, "is to do the will of him who sent me and to finish his work." John 4:34. His prayers were heard because he yielded his life in reverence to God.

When you obey God, you honor your father in heaven. God's word says this. "Honor your father and mother— which is the first commandment with a promise — that it may go well with you and that you may enjoy long life on the earth." Eph 6:1-3. When Jesus taught his disciples to pray, he taught the first commandment with promise was to address your father with honor and respect. In hallowed be thy name, Jesus pointed out that your Fathers name was to be treated as if he and his name were sacred. In his own prayers, (John 17) Jesus referred to his father as Holy Father who was righteous.

Have you ever seen an unruly child who says, "you can't make me do that, you're not my father?" The boy said that you're not my father and you can't make me do that. This boy knows who his father is and did not recognize your authority. It's a relationship of love to obey your father but isn't that what you say to God when you disobey him? The honor that you give to God is only a part of the overall way you treat God but it is the way you treat God that shows the honor you have for him.

Jesus said, "These people honor me with their lips, but their hearts are far from me." Matt 15:8. Good intentions are promises not kept, but that is when you are not true to your word. People who say one thing and do another are those who honor God with their lips on Sunday but blend so well into the world that you can't tell them apart. God watches over your life but to worship God in spirit and in truth your prayers must agree what you say and do. You can't con God because he is with you 24 hours a day 7 days a week and prayer is not lip service. When you tell God that you will do something for him, you better do it.

Be a King in the King's eye.

You are one of many Kings that serve a risen Savior who is the King of kings. God wants you to know how to rule your life as a king would. A king will make thousands of decisions in his lifetime and you will make choices as long as you live. You can go into the throne room of grace without fear that your father will run you out or that he does not have time to hear your need. You can ask him what you want and it will be given to you. However, do you think like a king and can you command God to do a miracle? Paul said that God is able to do more than you can think or imagine but have you asked God to save the county or the state you live in. God said, "I am the LORD, the God of all mankind. Is anything too hard for me?" Jer 32:27, and that, "Whatever you ask for in prayer, believe that you have received it, and it will be yours." Mark 11:24. God has told you that he is able to answer even the toughest of prayers and he will do it when you believe you have his answers. Therefore, you should ask God for the impossible and expect him to answer your prayer.

Kings make decisions for others and they expect their commands carried out. Their commands tell you what their goals are but not always how to achieve it. Try to approach God in the same way for God is creative and has his way to do things. Don't try to show or tell God how to answer your prayer because he knows what he is doing. Be a king and let God decide how to carry out your commands.

Is there a special way to pray?

There is no magic formula to prayer or a unique way you have to talk to God? God wants his name to be treated with respect and held sacred in your eyes. Anyone can go to God to repent of his or her sin but a son can have all his needs met according to his riches in glory. Jesus said, "Ask and it will be given to you; seek and you will find; knock and the door will be opened to you." Luke 11:9. All one can do is to ask with the expectation that God will give you your needs.

There is no special way to pray but the shape of your spirit will hamper your prayers? Sin will hamper your prayers from being answered and that is a sure sign that you need to do a spiritual check up. Action speaks louder than words and you need to look at what you have been doing. If you can not find sin in your life, ask God to let you know what is wrong for the sole reason that you want to repent and make things right.

Stopwatch prayer.

Stopwatch prayer seems to be a strange way to speak of prayer but that is what a few men say you need to do. A small number of men govern their prayer life by the time they spend in prayer. They think you should spend at least one to two hours a day in prayer. God appreciates your prayers no matter the length of your prayer.

Look to Jesus who taught you to pray in Luke 11, he said the phrase, "and when you pray." The word, when, tells you that prayer is voluntary and it is your desecration whether or not you pray. However, habits make your prayer life more productive. The point is that you need to spend time with God in prayer and not regulate prayer as a formal rite. The time you spend with God in prayer is solely up to you and the needs you have. Since God lives in you, you can go to your father anytime of the day. You don't have to set aside an hour a day to spend with your father but you should make it a habit to pray daily for your own good.

Men do things to discipline their lives and a set time to read and pray. You can always plan what you are going to pray about. You can make a prayer list, keep a journal and still pray from your heart. Still wanting to pray for an hour does sound does like a good goal but it may be difficult to manage when all you are doing is filling up a time slot. Think for a minute, did your parents ever demand that you spend an hour each day with them so you could tell them what went on that day? Each child of God has needs that fit his or her life style and God wants you to love him of your free will. Living by the standards others have does not work for most people and when it is all said and done, may ruin your prayer life. Trying to be super spiritual may do more harm than good.

Setting your clock to pray for a specific length of time can render your prayers to a formal thesis, loosing the zeal that you need to be effective prayer warrior.

God said, "For my house will be called a house of prayer for all nations." Isa 56:7. Paul said. "Don't you know that you yourselves are God's temple and that God's Spirit lives in you?" 1 Cor 3:16. Your body is the current house of prayer and God is in you 24 hours a day, 7 days a week. Prayer is not for show and tell but you can make prayer into a formal exercise of futility like the Pharisees of Jesus day. Instead, use your time in prayer to build a personal relationship with God.

God has always worked with men as their spirit moved them so God will not force you to be a prayer warrior. You are free to set goals that govern your prayer life but the object of prayer is for you to know God. As God can stir your heart to move by faith your prayer should stir God to answer your prayer.

CHAPTER 22

Associating With Friends And Family Of God

> Let us not give up meeting together, as some are in the habit of doing, but let us encourage one another- and all the more as you see the Day approaching.
>
> Heb 10:25.

Christ did not go to his father's house on the Sabbath day to be a bump on a log. He went to hear the words of God exhorted, worship his father and to pray. Today, people meet at the church at 4th and Maple for the same reasons. In this context the church is called the House of God and people still meet God there for the first time. The church is made up of God's children and other friends that meet in his house. You may think of it as going home for Sunday dinner since you go to dine with your family.

In Bible times the church was the center of the Jewish life and the school that taught the people the law of God. The church was known as a synagogue, and as a house of instruction. It was a place where the people could gather and the law of God was argued in detail and studied with zeal. Anyone of age could stand up to read from the scrolls and tell what it meant to them. Christ was twelve when he spent three days at a synagogue to talk about matters of the law. Later in life he stood up to read from Isaiah and he spoke with power.

To some, going to church can be a social event of their week. The ladies need to show off new clothes and the kids come with their parents. The deacons are expected to be there and salesmen want to be seen so they often go to be known. The mayor and councilmen have their reason to attend. Some can't say why they are there but the largest part of the congregation wants to honor their father and lift him up as God.

Going to church is another way to spend time with God and associate with their brothers and sisters in Christ and a few friends that were drawn by God. Church is more than going to at a place of worship for it is made up of God's children that gather to praise and thank God as a group. The Church is the family unit of God that comes together to hear the word of God exalted and God will bless you when you go to church to hear the truth.

Knowing God's law.

God said to Israel, get rid of your moral filth and wash your clothes then meet me at the base of the mountain in three days. With his people prepared to meet God they stood at the foot of the mountain and God spoke to his people giving his law from his own mouth. Then God appeared to Israel and gave his laws to give his people a respect for his law so that they would be sure to obey him. This grand event gave men a reason to remember an awesome God and keep his law. This is what God did to get their attention.

> "On the morning of the third day there was thunder and lightning, with a thick cloud over the mountain, and a very loud trumpet blast. Everyone in the camp trembled. Then Moses led the people out of the camp to meet with God, and they stood at the foot of the mountain."
>
> Exod 19:16-17.

This was a sight to behold, so awesome that all Israel shook in their shoes for they had seen the glory of God. With their ears they heard the majestic voice of God and no one could question that the word they heard was from God. God wanted men to hear his law and learn to revere him as long as they lived. God gave Israel the standards that he lives by and a set of laws for all men to love their creator and their peers.

It's evident that God wants his kids to wear clean clothes. God has always provided clothing for those he loves, for Adam it was the skins that covered his body. Robes were given to the priest's and the Bride of Christ has a gown of pure white linen. God gives clean clothes for you to wear, but in the process of daily life you get them soiled. When God said to wash your clothes and get rid of your moral filth, he was saying that he did not want you to wear clothes soiled with sin. Because God is a Spirit, he can see things like the sin in your heart that you can not. "Fine linen, bright and clean, was given her to wear. (Fine linen stands for the righteous acts of the saints.)." Rev 19:8. Finally Jesus said, "Blessed are those who wash their robes, that they may have the right to the tree of life and may go through the gates into the city." Rev 22:14. Washing your robes is something you must do so anytime you soil your robes be quick to clean them.

Why go to church?

"Assemble the people—men, women and children, and the aliens living in your towns—so they can listen and learn to fear the LORD your God and follow carefully all the words of this law." Deut 31:12. God has commanded that you assemble as a body to hear his law. He wants you to learn how to respect him and to obey him his law, for in doing so God is able to groom you into a mature person that can love as he does.

Jesus is the center and catalyst of Christian life and the church helps you to face the world. You may be tired of what the world has to offer and tired of the lies of the world. Tired of the boom box that screams of doom, and those who shout the Lord's name in vain, and your heart is aching when you know that the world doesn't want to serve God. You may hate the views that the world dumps on you and are weary of hearing the world's plea to have fun with their sin. However, like the psalmist said, it's when you walk into the house of God that your eyes are opened to their fate. That is when you see that they need to hear the good news more than ever before.

The church should have an influence on your life and an influence on the community it serves. One reason for the church is to exalt the word of God being a witness to all who have entered its doors. Still, it is a relief to find out that you are not going off your rocker and that others believe in God as you do. You can worship God as you want and find rest from the evil of the world. For a change you can be a fanatic and shout glory to God and not have eyes staring at you as if you were crazy.

The least the church should do is to support you in prayer. Let your needs be known to the church so the church knows how to pray for you. The church will add strength to your faith and you gain the strength of numbers when your plea is heard by God. God's house is a house of prayer for all of his people and your prayer should cast your cares on God with the strength of the church.

Each Christian is a part of God's family and the idea is to gather in one place to hear from your father. You may go and be quiet or you may participate in what is going on. The person that enjoys church the most goes to serve your needs and wants to help others.

The church will help you to grow.

Most churches have one main doctrine that teaches you how to have a relationship with God. A full gospel will tell you the whole plan of God. Leaving any part of his plan out may cause you to lack traits or skills that God wants you to have. The church is the tool that God uses to teach you all of his commands, and your Sunday school will go through the Bible on the average of once in five years. All of this helps you to know God better.

> Wake up! Strengthen what remains and is about to die, for I have not found your deeds complete in the sight of my God.
>
> Rev 3:2.

Some in the church fail to grow and are childish or stagnant but God wants to see you mature. God wants you to bud and ripen as a man that he designed you to be. Revival is God's alarm system to wake you up. First it lets you spend more time with God than you usually do, this puts your mind back in focus for the things of God. Secondly, it lets you see things you failed to see under your regular pastor. To grow you need to spend time in the truth and apply God's word to the way you live. Revival is a shake up time when you see a need for new commitments. However, commitments are short lived and most revert to their old ways in two to three weeks.

Most people stray from their plans and you will stray from the word when life tugs on you. Don't go to church to see what others do, but find a way to be of help with those who need help. Check out the ideas heard at church, because you have to work your salvation with God. Still you can miss parts of God's plan that you need to know and a full gospel church, in time, will help you to see the parts you miss. Granted, what you hear may step on your toes but that may be because you have strayed from the path God wants you on.

Your role in the church.

The church should make leaders in Christ and to grow as a church you should rise in the ranks. Be faithful in the work of the church and grow as the needs of the church develop. God has a big job for you to do that may take an hour or two a week to do. Some of the jobs give you the experience you need to move on to other jobs that require more trust. God needs reliable people that finish the jobs they start.

Working with the leaders leads to other jobs. You can build trust with the leaders by doing jobs that they want done. Whether it is in the work force or in the church, good workers are hard to find. However, being lax at any job will keep you from rising in the ranks and this is work that you do of your free will.

"Are all apostles? Are all prophets? Are all teachers? Do all work miracles?" 1 Cor 12:29. These are the building gifts of the church and you may have one of these gifts. Whatever your gifts, use them to God's glory and use them faithfully. However, most jobs in the church have no acclaim to them and still need to be done. Some of those jobs are out side the church walls and your pastor would be glad to take you along when he visits the sick. Visitors do not show up at the church door in the numbers you would like to see, so you must invite them. The church will grow, but you need to put your skills to do the work that will result in church growth. Within the church, you can sweep the floor, fold the bulletins, usher, greet, teach, take care of the children, lead the worship and pray for the sick. The most important job in the church is the one you have and God will honor you for it.

The Academy of Kings.

The goals of the church are to disciple and teach you how to live. The church trains God's children to live by the laws that God rules his kingdom by. You may want to consider that Christ is a king who uses tutors to teach his sons how to rule in his place. As you grow in Christ, you should be more like him. The logic is simple since a king can be a tyrant or noble, however, a noble will handle things with grace when a tyrant will not. God wants his sons to be taught how to be noble and to show his grace to anyone who walks into the house of God.

God wants you to know the difference between good and evil. God takes interest in the choices you make and then ponders your choices to see how you are growing. A king is known by the way he rules and when you make choices, your choices affect the lives of others. God teaches you to do things his way, so you can be just, fair, and right with those you rule with.

The word seen by other eyes.

Pastors and teachers are a gift from God that offer you a view that is not yours. They may spend weeks to give a series of views on the same subject or a new subject each week. God will shed his light on his word to them in a different way than he did for you. You may not agree with his beliefs but he is doing the job God has given him to do. Think of God's word as a spoke to a wheel. Does that mean that they should see God's word from the spoke of the wheel as you do? You see the hub of the wheel from one spoke and they see the hub from another. That gives you a good reason to check what you have heard for the truth and turn the wheel to see what they saw. The object is to see the word of God for its truth and that you will have the edge you need to grasp the prize when the race is over.

A church of sinners.

God says that all have sinned and fall short of the glory of God. The church you go to is not perfect and you are in the same boat as those who attend church. God advises you not to judge others, especially when you see church member's involved in sin outside the church. If you look hard enough, you will see sin in each person that goes to church. Church is for the sinner as much as it is for those who are saved by the grace of God.

Repentance is a constant effort to keep your life pure from sin and change the way you live. You may not know it, when you repent you turn away from sin or shun evil. The word of God is spoken at church but that may be when God comes to inspect your clothes. To you, God's word is the spic and span that washes your clothes and church may be the only time that you get to hear his word. That may be all it takes to get you to wash your robes from sin. "Blessed are those who wash their robes, that they may have the right to the tree of life and may go through the gates into the city." Rev 22:14.

The church of one accord.

The church must learn to work as one if the church is to have an effect on the public. Not all want to go door to door but God gave men many talents. "We have different gifts, according to the grace given us." Rom 12:6, and not all of you have gifts to lead the church. Remember, some of the members will do anything for the Lord and others will only do what they want to do. Each member will do as he or she pleases even when the church has a plan to grow.

The members of your church need to come up with a plan that they can agree to do at least a portion of it. If one member draws up the plan, those who dissent will not work for those goals. God said this to the church. "I appeal to you, brothers, in the name of our Lord Jesus Christ, that all of you agree with one another so that there may be no divisions among you and that you may be perfectly united in mind and thought." 1 Cor, 1:10. Perhaps all it takes is for your church to have a meeting for the purpose of drawing up a plan. The church has to decide what their community needs in line with the needs of God. Ask questions to find out what the assets that the church has and what the members are willing to do. What ever the outreach plan is, the members of the church should play an important part of seeking the lost.

Start out with a goal that the church can agree with and fill the jobs with people who can agree to be a part of the plan. Those in leadership roles should commit to lead the plan and assist with the work for the church goals. Leave some of the jobs for the members who will do anything for the Lord in reserve. All jobs have procedures that work, so train your members how to do the work. "Commit to the LORD whatever you do, and your plans will succeed." Prov 16:3. Do everything that you know to do to make the plan a success.

Life with God.

God wants you to be productive in every area of your life and live without sin. Christ was sent to earth as a man to restore all men to God and your sins was bound to the body of Christ at the cross. To

God, Christ was your sin and his death paid the penalty for your sins. You are now able to have a life with God based on the death and blood of Christ. With the new life that God has given you he has a plan for you to serve others.

There are times that you have to yield to the needs of others to have any harmony of life. The doctor wants you to take your pills, the cop does not want you to speed and God wants you to live a holy life. You need to agree with those in authority and the terms that others make so you can live. The same rule works with God and to be born again, you agreed to obey God. God must see deeds that agree with your word to obey him so he will know the truth. Above all else God wants you to keep your word and see you serve him in spirit and in truth.

God is your help no matter where who you are, and what you are doing. Take advantage of the time he gives you to know the one and only true God. God wants to know you, so spend your time with God. Read and study his word, pray for the wisdom you need and talk things over with God. Associate with other Christians like yourself and take part in his plan of salvation. God does not want anyone to perish especially you who he loves deeply.

CHAPTER 23

Do You Know God's Will For Your Life?

How do you answer anyone who wants to know what God's will is for them when you don't know. You can tell them what you think but that won't help them. The walk with God is a process and you have to work out your salvation with God because his will for your life is between you and God. However, Christians reach a point that they want to do more to please God. God said.

> "I will put my Spirit in you and move you to follow my decrees and be careful to keep my laws."
>
> Ezek 36:27.

Make a study of two words (moved and stirred) that may help you to know God's will. The spirit of

God will stir your heart into action and the desire to know God's will is proof of that. When you pray, ask God to stir your heart so you will know what he wants you to do for him. Open your eyes to see what is going on in your lives. Look at the needs of others and take steps of faith based on what you see.

You need skills before God will send you into his field to work. In Matt 25:15. Jesus told the story of a noble that went away to be a king. Before he left, he put a few of his servants in charge and each was given a sum that agreed with their skills. Being a stern man he made each liable for the use of his money. They knew before he left that he wanted to see how his money had increased when he returned.

God has big jobs to do and he needs you to do them. God has lofty ideas and goals that reach beyond what your mind can fathom. You have to do first things first, as growing to be like God is a process. You can do the work that God gives you but you can not be a Christian without God leading you. Being born again does not give you a degree in godliness and you must learn all you can about him. You must learn to work with God and accept what he does for you to be able to thank God for the work he does in your life. This is when you learn that there is so much that you can do and then you expect God to pick up the slack and do the jobs you can't.

All relationships have trust built into them but can God trust you to do the work he has for you to do? Like your boss, God has work he wants done and he does not want to hear excuses. God knows that you can only do so much and God wants the glory for the work you can not do.

Do you really want to know God's will?

The Bible does not tell you to start a ministry in Africa, or how to run a food bank. That may be your idea of what God wants you to do, but having a fear like this should tell you that you are not ready to do God's will. God will give you a craving to do his will and wanting to go shows your zeal to do God's will. Going to Africa or running a food bank are ways to spread the gospel when you think about it. A life without God will leave you in the dump, feeling worthless, but the love you have for God will show any man that his life is worth living. You have the skills to change the life of another when you do the will of God. You have the choice to make the difference with God's help.

How to know God's will?

Most of the people that I have talked with who say they know the will of God, say it all started with a feeling. They feel that God led them to do the job that they are doing. God was stirring their heart and they did what they were impressed to do. Do what you can for God and search the scriptures for advice. For example, "Whoever can be trusted with very little can also be trusted with much." Luke 16:10. God may use this principle to give you a role to play in his kingdom and you may want to do something to show God that you are faithful. If you feel that God is leading you to do something, step out in faith and do what you feel he is leading you to do. If the doors are opened be ready to take the next step. You may want to pray like Gideon who tested the Lord to know God's will. Ask God to open or close the doors that are before you.

You can not please God without faith and the step out in faith shows God that you are ready to do his will. If you are the Gideon type, ask God to let you know his will and ask him to confirm his will in as many ways as you need. Are you willing to step out on the limb and cut on the tree side? Are you willing to be laughed at if you are wrong? God will honor your faith and he will give you a desire to do his will.

God's call on my life.

A few years ago, I did a study on the Coming of Christ and I found a typewriter at a yard sale, which I bought. I did not know why at the time but for some reason I started to keep notes on that toy. The only way I could put my notes on paper was to hunt and peck since the right key was hard to find. I felt driven to type and learned that white out hides bad typing. I don't know why, but I wanted neat notes so I spent two to three hours typing just one page over. I was tough so I kept on typing.

My wife heard me typing and she types a hundred words a minute when I typed ten. She had to have said, Oh my God! He is driving me up the wall. One day, I told my wife that it would be nice to have a computer for my notes. I had seen a used one, but my wife said that it was a waste of money. To my surprise, three large boxes were under the Christmas tree that year. It was a new computer for me. Boy, I must have been good that year!

I have learned to love the gifts God has given to me by my wife. This machine saves time in retyping the page but it gave me fits at first. I kept finding the only key that don't belong on my keypad. Not knowing what I was doing, I lost much of what I just put into the computer and it made me wonder if it was worth it. I asked, what do I do now when I did not know what the computer would do. I could have save hours if I knew where the undo gadget was. I tried to read the book that came with the machine but a nerd wrote it. He spoke in terms I did not know and asked me to push buttons I couldn't find. The book might as well have been written in Arabic as much help as it was. That's when I knew what to do with that book. I put it back on the shelf, but at the same time I was at a loss to know how to do my work. Trial and error were the only way left to press onward even though I thought at the time that my wife gave this toy to get even with me.

My wife tried her best to help me but she did not know how to teach me a system she had never seen. She worked with a different system at work and my operating system made as much sense to her as it did to me. Then I used the system my wife said works the best. Push a key and see what happens and if that doesn't do the job, try another key. Believe me, it did not take long to know what key not to touch when it made a mess of what I was trying to do. Then there was a time when I was at my best crashing the system. I became known for saying, "What on earth did I do this time?" You know Murphy's law, if it could go wrong I did it, especially when nothing seemed to work.

I knew that I needed to learn how to use the computer if I was going to write a book. It took time to learn the skill to use it as a tool but I thrive on solving problems. My persistence and the resolve to master the computer and make it into a tool for God's will was my greatest strength. Well, things leveled out for a time and I began to hit the keys with the wise sayings of an old man that is, until I read what I wrote. It was the wise sayings of an old man proved just how wise I was. It did not take me long to cry out to God for help. I need you Lord, the ideas I put on paper doesn't make sense.

I started to write down my ideas of the coming of Christ. But that is when I realized that my subject had changed. The flow of ideas that came from God was not talking of his return. Then I wondered, did God have other ideas in mind. As I look back, I know that God kept me out of trouble because I am not up to par with all the beliefs of the church.

I found out that writing a book was not as easy as one would think. I was the kind of man that did not write well to begin with and flew by the seat of his pants. The plan for my life did not go beyond that of the scriptures and I did not have a plan that went farther than what I was going to do that day.

However, I was writing about the things I loved to do when it came to God's word. The people at church where I went came to me for the answers they needed and they knew that I had a grasp of the Bible. A part of the answer that I gave to them was that I urged them to read and study God's word for themselves. I felt good as I came to know God was using me for His glory and I enjoyed doing it.

I had a need in my life to do a job for Christ to the best of my ability. So I bought a book on writing made easy to teach myself to write. After reading the book I knew what was wrong. The book said that I needed a plan and I didn't have one. I said, plans are not my bag, if you know what I mean, when I prayed to God. God heard my prayer, and in less than a week the plans were in my mind, on paper and on the wall with flags and flying colors. Saying here I am! The answer was so strong that it was like shaking the ground. I knew the hand of God was there to give me a plan.

It took some time to learn God's wisdom and it meant that I had to start over. This time I knew that God was with me and the book began to take shape. The book doubled in content. Each time I edited my ideas the book became easier to read. There were times when the ideas came to a stop and I was writing the same things over and over. In addition, I found that I was putting words on paper that should have been left out of this book, and I was writing words that did not fit the needs of the book. I wrote too much on the wrong topics and too little on others. All this did was to tell me that I needed to edit the book again.

In the off times I learned how to work closer with God. It made me think that the prophets did the same things as I was doing when they wrote their letters to the church. They said so much in a short letter and I wanted this book to be like their letters. The ideas came to a stop when I strayed from the plan of the book. God was telling me to look at what I was doing, as if he were saying keep your mind on your work. It was like the only fumble of a football game that made the coach to go back to the basics and I was calling on God again for help.

I had to say that studying God's word was God's plan for your life and I wanted to show everyone the need for the mind of God. Still, this book had to prove my case and glorify God. If anything, this book has been a task that I have grown in. I know now that God will give me the power to do the things that I can not do alone. God used some skills I did not know I had, and I was using new skills that made people think. I know now that God prepared me for my life ahead. I have a future to look to. I also know that I still need to rely on God for his skills.

In my mind I could see this book in print, and in my mind I had a goal to aim for. If I expected to write a book I had to do what it takes to write one and keep my mind focused on the goal. The target was bigger than any goal I had ever had before but the job I was doing now had a purpose. A goal both

God and I wanted. I had a habit of leaving things undone in the past but for the first time I had a desire to finish this task like I have never known before. It's not my ego speaking when I say I have a belief that this book will be printed. I know that this is God's plan and I want God to have all the glory.

I have learned a great deal about God these last seven years and how to work with him. Most of the ideas in this book that I have used came to me before I heard them from other sources. Some of the ideas that I have used are new and others are not but I know they are from God. At times the ideas came faster than I could take them in but every part of the plan God had for me fell into place in his time. This book shows how God is working in me and I pray that he continue to do so, Lord knows I need him. Thank you Lord.

God showed me his will for my life and it has helped to make me into a better man of God. I am starting to see where I fit into his plan and that he wants to make me into a leader. I am a priest of his kingdom and some day I may be the man that God made me to be. I know that his plan will make it happen and the same is true of your life. I did not tell my story for ego's sake, especially when I think that God wants you to see what I have seen. Bits and pieces of my testimony reflect the strengths of God. The strength of influence of faith and endurance and giving all I have stood out in this book. Reread the book and you will see those strengths.

My hope is you will see that God gave you the skills to be like him too. The workers in God's field are few but God would love to have you as one of them. For me, my faith is in God and I know that the best is yet to come.

My prayer

O LORD. I have finished the book you have given me to write and it is time to commit this work to you.

I have written the ideas you gave to me in this book. You sent me to tell your plan to your church so no one would perish but to be a strong vibrant Christian. I have done all I know to do to see that this book is published. I place this book into your hands and I commit it to you and your work on earth. I ask you to bless the work of the publisher and the time the reader has so it may bear fruit in the lives of your children.

LORD, I want others to know that this has been an exciting time in my life. I know that a plan to promote your work lies ahead of me. Give me the strength to press on to the goal that you want me to reach. My greatest hope is that those who read this book will use their time to know you and that they will open their hearts to seek you with all their heart. Let this book be used for your glory.

In Jesus name. A men.

About The Author

Kenneth Dobbin was born in March 1944 in Brocton, New York, and graduated from Brocton Central High School in 1962. Ken left New York to serve in the U.S. Air Force as an aircraft mechanic. After he was discharged, Ken moved to Columbus and twelve years later to Marysville, Ohio, where he has lived since 1978. During that time he met his wife, Kareen, of thirty-four years. They raised a daughter, Kimberly, who is married to Chris Donnal. They are the parents of Ken's granddaughter, Kayla, who is twelve years old.

He made a living as a carpenter and framed houses for twenty-two years. Then he met the Lord, who changed Ken's life. He taught Sunday school for four years at Christian Assembly and served on the church board for eight of the fifteen years he attended there. He built an addition onto the First Baptist Church of Marysville. He is now attending the Church of the Nazarene out of respect for his father. Ken is currently serving as his guardian.

Ken has been a Christian for the last twenty years, and during that time he has seen a number of people known to be Christians who could not find the book of Haggai. That bothers him. In addition, some have come to Ken asking what he thinks the Bible says and seeking answers to other questions. Ken's hope is that this book will make the difference in the world and that the ideas he presents will positively affect those who read it. While Ken calls his book *Do You Know God?*, he has committed the book to the glory of God. His hope is that God will honor the work that He has called him to do.

For those of you that want a study guide for *Do You Know God?*, Ken has prepared a booklet containing six hundred questions pertinent to knowing God. To request the booklet, send six dollars and your return address to:

Do You Know God?
17444 Paver Barnes Rd.
Marysville, Ohio 43040

Printed in the United States
1386900001B/55-255